CrossTalk:
COMMUNICATING IN A MULTICULTURAL WORKPLACE

Sherron B. Kenton, Ph.D.

Deborah Valentine, M.S.

Foreword by C. Richard Yarbrough
Managing Director of Communications
Atlanta Committee for the Olympic Games

Prentice Hall
Upper Saddle River, New Jersey 07458

Library of Congress Cataloging-in-Publication Data

Kenton, Sherron B., 1949–
    Crosstalk : communicating in a multicultural workplace / Sherron
  B. Kenton, Deborah Valentine ; foreword by C. Richard Yarbrough.
        p.   cm.
  Includes bibliographical references and index.
  ISBN 0-13-577628-7
  1. Communication in management.   2. Intercultural communication.
  3. Diversity in the workplace--Management.   I. Valentine, Deborah,
  1948– .   II. Title.
  HD30.3.K455   1997   96-27173
  302.3'5--dc20   CIP

Editorial/Production Supervision,
    Interior Design, and Electronic Paging: *Naomi Sysak*
Acquisitions Editor: *Elizabeth Sugg*
Cover Director: *Jayne Conte*
Manufacturing Buyer: *Ed O'Dougherty*
Managing Editor: *Mary Carnis*
Marketing Manager: *Danny Hoyt*
Director of Production: *Bruce Johnson*

Published by Prentice-Hall, Inc.
A Simon & Schuster Company
Upper Saddle River, New Jersey 07458

Printed in the United States of America

10   9   8   7   6   5   4   3   2   1

ISBN 0-13-577628-7

Prentice-Hall International (UK) Limited, *London*
Prentice-Hall of Australia Pty. Limited, *Sydney*
Prentice-Hall Canada Inc., *Toronto*
Prentice-Hall Hispanoamericana, S.A., *Mexico*
Prentice-Hall of India Private Limited, *New Delhi*
Prentice-Hall of Japan, Inc., *Tokyo*
Simon & Schuster Asia Pte. Ltd., *Singapore*
Editora Prentice-Hall do Brasil, Ltda., *Rio de Janeiro*

DEDICATION

For my parents, Mackie and Ben Bienvenu, who told me I could do anything.
For my daughter, Hillary Tolle, so she will know that anything is possible.
And, of course, for Ken.

SHERRON B. KENTON

For the best family an author could ever want: Howard, Ann Larie, and William.

DEBORAH VALENTINE

Contents

CHAPTER 4:   WHAT IF YOUR AUDIENCE HAS ROOTS IN THE ASIAN CULTURE?   71

FOREWORD

My first awareness of the importance of international communication occurred in early 1984. A public corporation with whom I was affiliated was in the process of getting listed on the various stock exchanges around the world, including Japan. The individual in charge of the process was an assistant vice president, and he took with him to Tokyo his top assistant, who in the management hierarchy was a director-level manager.

Before their trip, they dutifully had business cards translated into Japanese, but they found during their meetings that the Japanese were referring their questions and comments to the director-level manager and not to his boss. No matter how hard they tried, they found their hosts maintained the most interest in the subordinate of the two. It was not until their return to the United States that they discovered the translation of the business cards had made the director-level manager a "director" of the operation and his boss, the assistant vice president, an "assistant."

Welcome to multicultural communications!

I was reminded of that incident when I read **CrossTalk**, this marvelous new book by Sherron Kenton and Deborah Valentine. In addition, I have had similar experiences brought home to me almost daily as managing director of communications for the Atlanta Committee for the Olympic Games. My only complaint is that they didn't write this book sooner.

As I have traveled around the world in preparation for the Centennial Olympic Games, I have found that most Americans (particularly those of my generation) are oblivious to other cultures, and in this shrinking universe in which we find ourselves, that is an attitude we, as a nation, can ill afford in the future. Economists say that there are fast becoming only two markets in which to compete: local and international. And if we are to compete successfully in the international marketplace, we had better learn the rules. First and foremost, we must learn to communicate with people who have a culture different from ours, and that is where you will find **CrossTalk** invaluable.

No longer can we assume that everyone thinks as we do, acts as we do, has the same value system we do, or even enjoys the same things we do. Nor should we make the mistake that when we speak or write, we are communicating. Communications involves the *exchange* of ideas.

And now the good news. Authors Kenton and Valentine have successfully withstood the temptation to take an important subject like multicultural communications and write a complicated treatise about it. **CrossTalk** is easy to read, and that is very much to their credit. Come to think of it, that is why they are such superb communicators, and why I can enthusiastically recommend this book to you.

As we prepare to greet a new century and a new world order, many things we have taken for granted in the past will be forever changed. One thing won't change, however, and that is our need to communicate with one another.

You may be holding the most important book on that subject that you will ever read—or need.

C. Richard Yarbrough
Managing Director—Communications
Atlanta Committee for the Olympic Games

ACKNOWLEDGMENTS

We are most grateful to the following individuals for their contributions to *CrossTalk: Communicating in a Multicultural Workplace.*

Dick Yarbrough, for his time and generosity in writing our foreword

Reviewers

- Dr. Norma Carr-Ruffino
- Dr. Thomas Fernandez
- Dr. Evelyn Pierce
- Dr. Paul Timm

Chapter reviewers

* Chapter 2: Dr. Karen Hegtvedt
* Chapter 3: Harbert Bernard, Karen Jones, and Andrea Scott
* Chapter 4: Dr. David Shaner and Rumiko Mori
* Chapter 5: Kristin Lindsey, Lorraine Polvinale, Liliana Roman, and Elsa Valdiviezo de Baules

Contributors

- Clients who provided brilliant applications of our models
- Foreign students for culture-specific examples
- International businesspeople who consented to be interviewed
- Ken Kenton and Howard Valentine for sharing their valuable professional contacts
- Jim Sitlington for his wisdom, encouragement, and humor

Our computer experts, especially Nancy Stauffer and Darrell Felton

Our Emory colleagues for moral support, especially Dr. Nick DeBonis, Andrea Hershatter, Earl Hill, Donis Leach, Heather Mugg, Nancy Roth Remington, and Dr. Greg Waymire

Our supportive colleagues in the Association for Business Communication and the Management Communication Association.

Research assistants

- Amy Kane-Stanley
- Jean de Silva
- Lisa Millar
- Katie Proctor
- Erin Nicholson

And last but really first: Our incredible Prentice Hall team:

- Senior Editor Elizabeth Sugg, who always believed in us
- Production Editor Naomi Sysak, who read our minds
- Copyeditor Robert Fiske
- Carole Horton

Do you know someone who could have written this?

> *My professional peers consider me to be a successful manager. However, I find myself in a position at work where I am not as effective as I want to be. There was a time when I believed that I could motivate any subordinate or persuade any client assigned to me.*
>
> *In the past few years, the faces have changed. My office and my clients' offices include Asians and Latinos and African Americans and women where there used to be mostly white men. Not too long ago, everyone at work looked and talked a lot like I do.*
>
> *I'm an educated, open-minded guy with years of work experience, but my experience doesn't seem to apply with people who are so different from me. I consider myself a good communicator, but I'm missing something when I try to persuade or manage people from so many different cultures.*
>
> *What I need is a quick but credible reference to help me get ahead of my competitors. It doesn't seem to exist! What do you recommend?*

WHY WE WROTE THIS BOOK

In 1995, the Census Bureau reported that in 1994 nearly one in eleven U.S. residents was foreign born. In 1990, *Time* magazine predicted the following percentages of people would enter the U.S. workforce before the year 2000:

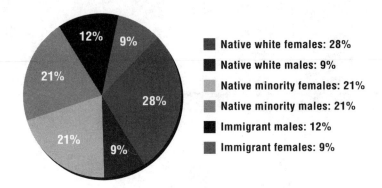

Native white females: 28%
Native white males: 9%
Native minority females: 21%
Native minority males: 21%
Immigrant males: 12%
Immigrant females: 9%

In addition, as technology advances, our business world continues to interconnect, with Americans investing more than $486 million in other countries, according to the U.S. Bureau of Economic Analysis, Survey of Current Business, July 1993.

As a result of increasing relationships with individuals whose culture is different from our own, our communication challenges grow proportionately greater. The response from the academic community has been to inundate the industry with an excess of complicated theories and strategies and models about communication in many different situations, in many different forms, with many different people. The result is too much information that is too complicated and too difficult to apply.

We offer, instead, one straightforward, strategic model for effective business communication. The **CrossTalk** Communication Model applies to writing, speaking, interviewing, and small group interaction. We then apply this flexible model to different situations with different people through understanding the cultural variables of each target group.

Our purpose is to make it easier and more effective for workplace professionals to speak, write, interview, or meet with other business professionals whose cultural backgrounds differ from their own.

We begin with these assumptions:

- Most of our readers were born or live or work in the United States. We consider ourselves American, and yet most of us are the product of a blend of cultures.
- A large proportion of our potential readers' cultural roots are European.
- The major audiences with whom our readers communicate have cultural roots that are European, African, Asian, or Latino.

Therefore, we have the following goals:

- To assist our readers in understanding their own cultures, particularly in terms of communication behaviors

- To help our readers become more aware of and sensitive to cultural differences in communication
- To present one basic communication model that is easy to use no matter what culture or mix of cultures you are addressing
- To enhance the applications to specific cultures with additional information on gender differences in workplace communication
- To illustrate the model and its applications with relevant examples from business situations

HOW THIS BOOK IS ORGANIZED

We have structured **CrossTalk** as follows:

CHAPTER 1:   THE CrossTalk COMMUNICATION MODEL

We offer one straightforward, strategic model for effective business communication that can be applied to writing, speaking, interviewing, and small group interaction. The resulting Kenton Credibility Model assesses perceived credibility.

CHAPTERS 2 THROUGH 5:   APPLICATIONS OF THE CrossTalk COMMUNICATION MODEL WITH AUDIENCES WITH DIFFERENT CULTURAL BACKGROUNDS

As a speaker, writer, interviewer, or meeting facilitator, you are faced with a multitude of audiences with cultural backgrounds that are different from your own. This book enables you to identify the cultural background of these receivers of your oral and written messages and then to specifically apply each point of the model to that individual or group.

Obviously, there are gender differences in all cultures. However, following the lead of Norma Carr-Ruffino in *Managing Cultural Differences* (Thomson Executive Press, 1996), we are addressing gender within the framework of our discussion of audiences with roots in the European culture (Chapter 2). In the United States, the majority of workers have roots in the European culture, much of which has evolved into what we generally consider to be the American culture.

In addition, the chapters that apply the **CrossTalk** Model to audiences with roots in African (Chapter 3), Asian (Chapter 4), and Latino (Chapter 5) cultures contain "gender notes" (🌰) at appropriate points throughout the application of the model.

Finally, we recognize that differences that affect communication exist *within* the major cultures. Therefore, each chapter includes information about these differences as "intracultural notes." (☯)

APPENDIXES

In keeping with our purpose of providing a quick reference and a credible source, the appendixes provide charts and examples to supplement the material in the chapters.

HOW TO USE THIS BOOK

Read the first chapter. You may race through thinking, "I know that," or "I do that." Good. That means you are a basically successful communicator with education, experience, and common sense. Keep in mind, however, that even one or two new ideas can make the competitive difference for your career.

Now, think about your day tomorrow. Whom will you manage or motivate or persuade? With this book, you can be better prepared to communicate with the following audiences:

- Men and women with roots in the European culture
- Men and women with roots in the African culture
- Men and women with roots in the Asian culture
- Men and women with roots in the Latino culture

Chapters 2 through 5 offer pragmatic applications of the **CrossTalk** Communication Model for these groups who will receive your oral and written messages.

The appendixes contain worksheets, examples, and other culture-specific information for quick referencing.

IN SUMMARY

We wrote this book because business managers and executives with excellent communication skills are highly valued in today's workplace. But the corporate environment has evolved into a complex and challenging arena staffed by increasingly diverse personnel. "Knowing the rules" or "getting the facts" is not enough.

CrossTalk: Communicating in a Multicultural Workplace gives you what you want so that you can do what you need to do: manage, motivate, and persuade people who look and think and sound different from you.

CHAPTER 1

THE CROSSTALK COMMUNICATION MODEL

We received this letter from a former client:

> *After being promoted to a regional management position, I am suddenly and acutely aware of how different my colleagues are from me. In addition, my company is expanding overseas, and my new job description may include some international responsibilities.*
>
> *In your Strategic Communications Workshop, you taught me not to assume or stereotype when I analyzed my target audience, but everyone seems to come from such different backgrounds, such diverse cultures. I have to select and organize information to motivate and manage and persuade these diverse audiences. I wish I could remember everything you said in class...*

The increasingly multicultural environment where we live and work creates a proportionately complex communication challenge. Our employers expect us to communicate effectively in complex situations to people who are often very different from ourselves. This does not have to be an overwhelming responsibility.

Some academics and rhetoricians would have us believe that each situation, purpose, audience, or medium requires a separate, unique, and confusing communication model. The truth, however, is that there is only one basic model for effective communication.

This is it: one strategic model for professional, managerial, and corporate communication. The **CrossTalk** Communication Model and your common sense are all you need to be an effective communicator in a multicultural business environment. An understanding of this model and its applications will allow you to be more credible and persuasive when you present, write, interview, or interact in teams and groups.

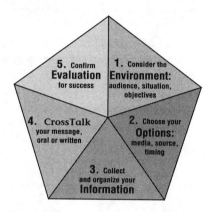

CONSIDER THE ENVIRONMENT

The environment of your communication includes the target audience, the existing situation, and your desired objectives. You need a thorough understanding of all three at the very beginning of your communication process, whether you are planning a first-quarter report to the board of directors, a sales presentation to representatives of a Japanese conglomerate, or simply a meeting with your secretary.

You may have difficulty assessing which actually comes first; the situation often motivates the communication, but that situation is rarely independent of your objectives and the individuals who will receive the message. Therefore, your analysis of audience, situation, and objectives is often simultaneous. However, you must learn to look at the different parts before you get a clear picture of how they work together.

Since the focus of this book is the challenge of communicating with individuals who are different from you, we will start with an analysis of your audience.

ANALYZE YOUR AUDIENCE

Your target audience is the individual or group who receives your written or oral message. Perfunctory audience analysis is practically automatic for most communicators, but this shallow evaluation is rarely sufficient. The biggest mistakes are generalizing and assuming, neither of which is effective, and both of which create greater misunderstanding.

Identify all of your potential audiences, and learn specific details about each of them. After you read the following descriptions, use the Audience Analysis Worksheet (Appendix B) to facilitate a thorough record of your examination of all of your target audiences.

Identify all potential audiences: primary, hidden, and decision makers. These can overlap, and there may be no hidden audience at all, but often we neglect the less obvious ones. Your primary audience is the actual individual(s) to whom you speak or write. Your hidden audience is an indirect receiver of your message. These individual(s) may not be directly connected with the actual communication purpose or process but may have some power over you; that is, their evaluation of your communication may somehow affect you or your job. The decision maker is your most important audience, even though this audience may rely on secondhand information from your primary audience.

FOR EXAMPLE

When Lynn Vincent presents to an internal client in her telecommunications company, her **primary audience** is sitting in front of her—members of the Southwest Sales group. Her **hidden audience** is a representative from Nippon Telephone and Telegraph who is exploring joint ventures in the United States (he also may be scouting talent). The **decision maker** is the vice president of Southwest Sales, who missed the presentation and will therefore depend on information from his employees.

Investigate and learn about each audience.   Be very careful to avoid generalizing and assuming as you focus on **facts, attitudes, wants,** and **concerns.**

Include both professional and personal **facts,** such as age, gender, education, job responsibilities and status, civic and religious affiliations, knowledge of your topic, and, of course, cultural background. Remember: The longer you have worked with people, the more you should know about them.

FOR EXAMPLE

When Jack Robins was asked to speak at the downtown Houston Rotary Club, he remembered that his father had belonged to a similar civic organization and assumed that all these men's groups were about the same.

Robins was surprised. He planned his presentation for a group of Texas oil men but delivered it to a male and female audience of top-level business professionals with roots in the Latino, African, Native-American, and Asian cultures. Robins was significantly less than successful because he did not learn the **facts** about his audience.

Everything we say about audience analysis should make you more comfortable in your communication skills. As a result, everything we tell you should boost your confidence, except this: We cannot safeguard you from a reluctant or hostile audience. You must therefore be aware of your audience's attitudes about you, about your topic, and about their actually being there as a receiver of your message.

FOR EXAMPLE

Sherron Kenton teaches an annual Strategic Presentations Workshop for employees of the Atlanta Gas Light Company in Atlanta. Supervisors recommend participants for the workshop because they make presentations regularly, might speak at a company meeting soon, or are anticipating promotions.

As she analyzes her audience, Dr. Kenton asks herself, "What are their **attitudes about me?**" *They have no idea who I am or what I'm going to do to them.* (Strike one.) "What are their **attitudes about my topic** (giving a presentation)?" *Most people would rather be thrown into a pit with snakes than make a speech.* (Strike two.) "What are their **attitudes about their being here**?" *It's required.* (Strike three.)

She realizes that she has not even begun to speak, and yet she is facing challenges beyond simply organizing and delivering her material.

The realization that your audience would rather be somewhere else, doing something else, with someone else is not a confidence booster. It does, however, remind you to work very hard as you select, organize, and present your material.

The next step in audience analysis involves your determination of what information your audience should receive, that is, what they **want**. Unfortunately, we make too many communication decisions on the basis of what we think our audiences "need to know." What your audience *needs* to know may be very different from what they *want* to know. Until you tell them what they *want* to know, they may not be receptive to what they *need* to know to fulfill the purpose of your communication.

FOR EXAMPLE

Accounting clerks in the Finance Division of a regional community college in the Southeast filed discrimination grievances because they believed that positions had been unfairly filled. Their supervisors had administered the search processes based on the principle of "need to know"; that is, only the people who needed to know about the job openings, such as the human resource staff, were informed. The people who **wanted** to know were not told. They assumed the oversight was intentional.

The resulting grievance procedures impeded work effectiveness in the entire division.

Finally, recognize your audience's fears—the consistent, major **concerns** that your audience expresses. In most situations, this issue is compounded by multiple audiences with multiple concerns.

When Sid Walters, Director of Patient Care, Southside Hospital, addresses the executive committee, he must consider the diverse **concerns** of the vice presidents. Their individual "fears" may include cost, image, quality, safety, and many other situational considerations. Identifying the major concerns that each individual has consistently expressed in the past can save Walters valuable time and energy in preparation, writing, and speaking.

In summary, analyzing your audience may be the most important component of your entire communication process because every subsequent decision you make depends on your accuracy and attention to detail at this point.
Remember:

- Identify your primary, hidden, and decision-making audiences.
- Discover personal, professional, and cultural facts, avoiding generalizations.
- Be aware of their attitudes about you, your subject, and their being there.
- Determine what they *want* to know, over and above what they *need* to know.
- Recognize consistent concerns.

ANALYZE YOUR SITUATION

Identify and define the problem.   That sounds easy, but narrowing the issues is often difficult. Isolate the particular decision that precipitated action in the form of communication; that is, what is the distinct cause for the message you must now prepare? Specify the parameters, and reduce the situation to manageable proportions.

The delay from Howard Ramirez's external vendor creates problems with his clients, office staff, sales representatives, and even upper management at Coca-Cola. Ramirez must recognize how each of these audiences is specifically affected by the bottle manufacturer's failure to adhere to delivery schedules before he prepares the appropriate messages. Even though there is one **cause**, the resulting issues are all more complex, and Ramirez must manage them individually.

Evaluate the corporate culture surrounding the problem.   Although the term corporate culture is often difficult to define, professionals agree that the nebulous attitudes and norms shared by members of an organization guide their appropriate behavior. The culture can therefore affect the appropriateness of your communication decisions.

FOR EXAMPLE

Employees of a patriarchal organization like UPS are more likely to respond positively to a directive than are employees of an entrepreneurial organization like MCI.

Consider UPS's move from Greenwich, Connecticut, to Atlanta, Georgia, where an overwhelming number of employees made remarkable personal transitions in agreeing to relocate. The **corporate culture** at UPS had successfully established an environment where the "family" stayed together, and members of the family were accustomed to relying on authoritative father figures (in this case, senior management) to make decisions and disseminate information about carrying out those decisions.

Assess the external climate.   Be aware of what's going on in the specific industry and in related industries.

FOR EXAMPLE

Human resource consultant Amy Kane-Stanley often recommends outplacement services for employees in a downsizing organization. However, when she consulted with RES Steel regarding layoff procedures, she responded to the **external climate**, including a cyclical steel market in a geographical area with few other employment opportunities. As a result of this analysis, she suggested that RES Steel invest in job sharing and cross-training.

If you understand an idea, you can communicate it.

WARREN BUFFETT, CEO, BERKSHIRE-HATHAWAY

ANALYZE YOUR OBJECTIVES

Most messages, no matter how simple or apparently insignificant, encompass **three objectives: an overall goal, a specific purpose of the communication, and a hidden agenda.** (See example on page 7.)

The **overall goal**—the foundation for decisions about your objectives—derives from the mission statement of the organization. This philosophy should be inherent in any message that represents the organization.

The **specific purpose** of the communication depends on your needs and on your analysis of the target audience. Pay particular attention to your audience's level of knowledge about your topic.

Persuasion can be visualized as a continuum from 0 to 10, where 0 represents "I know nothing about this," and 10 represents "I'm ready to sign on the dotted

FOR EXAMPLE

Star Enterprise, an affiliate company of Texaco, publishes an Environmental Conservation Policy that states: *Star Enterprise will assure that its operations do not intentionally harm the health of employees, the general public, or the environment and will conduct its operations with full concern for the protection of public health and property from pollution of land, air, and water.*

Star Enterprise discovered a petroleum leak under its Fairfax, Virginia, sales terminal building in July 1991. W. M. Stanfield, District Operations Manager, immediately wrote a personal letter (dated July 26, 1991) to residents of the affected neighborhood. Key phrases and sentences, all of which apply the Environmental Conservation Policy and therefore reflect the **overall goal**, include:

- The protection of human health and safety has been, and will continue to be, our first priority.
- ...we have set up an extensive monitoring program to detect threats to public health.
- To preclude the possibility of a leak in the future, several operational safeguards are now in place....
- We are committed...to live up to the expectation of us to be...a responsible corporate citizen.

line!" Speakers and writers often assume that their audiences know more than they actually do and ask those audiences to move too quickly up the continuum.

Conversely, poor communicators sometimes keep selling after they should have closed the deal. Work to accurately access where your audience is, and then set a reasonable objective.

FOR EXAMPLE

After spending countless hours researching the potential for manufacturing a specific new polyurethane byproduct at Polyco International, Charlie Day persuaded his supervisors to request a slot on the agenda of the April Executive Committee meeting.

Confident of the byproduct's success, Day asked the committee to accept his suggestion. Although Day's reasoning was sound, the committee was prepared only to recognize opportunity (approximately 3 on a scale of 1 to 10); finalizing the decision on a specific byproduct was asking too much, too soon. Day's request was tabled until the July meeting, thus delaying his plan for at least three months.

Recognizing that his second attempt might be his last, Day evaluated his audience more carefully before the July meeting and determined that the members of the committee were interested in options but not ready to select one. Day therefore decided that his **specific purpose** would be for them to consider a concrete proposal at their October meeting, based on criteria agreed on in July.

By moving his audience a step at a time, Day's new byproduct was approved for production in October.

And finally, you have a **hidden agenda**, a personal goal to which you are aspiring. *Everybody* has one; it is perfectly normal. Each time you present or write or participate in a meeting, you have an opportunity to fulfill that additional purpose.

FOR EXAMPLE

Robert Michaels is regional sales manager for the national branch of a multinational manufacturing firm, but his **hidden agenda** is that he aspires to international responsibilities. He has many occasions to express his knowledge of the international market, such as company sales meetings, informal gatherings, and strategic planning sessions. Articulating a broad-minded, global perspective is likely to be noticed by Michaels' superiors, therefore, creating awareness of his interests when opportunities arise in the organization.

CHOOSE YOUR OPTIONS

Now that you understand your audience, situation, and objectives, you can explore the communication options available to you: how the message should be sent (**medium**), who should deliver the message (**source**), and when the message should arrive (**timing**).

MEDIA OPTIONS: HOW SHOULD THE MESSAGE BE SENT?

Modern technology is providing an almost daily increase in **media** options. In addition to the standard letter, memo, speech, interview, meeting, and telephone, we also have fax, e-mail, teleconferencing, and the ubiquitous "grapevine" to choose from when deciding **how the message should be sent**. Table 1 contains media options, along with some advantages of each choice.

Unfortunately, we often make media choices based on our own wants and needs, rather than those of our target audiences.

FOR EXAMPLE

Lois Puckett will do almost anything to avoid writing a memo. Her manager, however, hates to make decisions without written data. If Puckett tries to talk to him about her important proposal, she is likely to be disappointed in the outcome. If she writes him a well-supported memo that he can read when he chooses to, Puckett is more likely to receive a positive response. Prioritizing success over convenience, Puckett chooses the **media** option that her target audience prefers and writes the memo.

SOURCE OPTIONS: WHO SHOULD DELIVER THE MESSAGE?

When selecting the source—**the person to deliver your message**—the most important criterion is the perceived credibility of that source by your target audience. In other

TABLE 1.1 MEDIA OPTIONS AND THE ADVANTAGES OF EACH CHOICE

	PERSONAL	CONFIDENTIAL OR CONTROVERSIAL	LOW PREPARATION TIME	FAST DELIVERY TIME	CONVENIENT FOR RECEIVER	CONSISTENT MESSAGE	ACCURATE, PERMANENT RECORD	NONVERBAL INTERACTION	IMMEDIATE RESPONSE TO SENDER
SPEAKING (FROM CASUAL TO FORMAL)									
Grapevine	y		y	y	y			y	
Conversation	y	y	y	y				y	y
Interview	y	y		y				y	y
Phone call	y	y		y					y
Meeting				y		y		y	y
Teleconference				y		y	y (if recorded)	y	y
Formal presentation				y		y	y (if videotaped)	y	y
WRITING (FROM CASUAL TO FORMAL)									
E-mail	y	y	y	y	y	y	y		
Informal note or greeting card	y	y	y		y		y		
Memo	y	y	y		y	y	y		
Fax	y			y	y	y	y		
Letter	y	y			y	y	y		
Report		y			y (if succinct)	y	y		
Business card	y				y	y	y		y

The letter y indicates yes, this medium generally offers this advantage.

Also consider appropriateness of the medium for the message, cost of sending the message though this medium, what the receiver wants, and how accountable you are going to be for the message.

words, who will your audience perceive as having the most experience, power, and concern for them? Poor communicators will often make this decision based on their needs rather than on those of the receiver.

We naturally take ownership of a project and then want to see it personally through to completion by delivering the message ourselves. In truth, however, someone else may be more effective in presenting your message. Make this decision based on your knowledge of your target audience.

FOR EXAMPLE

The internal auditing division of a multinational paper company is comprised of a diverse range of employees. The internal clients that the division serves are even more diverse. In order to increase effectiveness and decrease barriers created by bias and perception, audit teams are designed to include at least one member (**source**) who will be immediately perceived as **credible** by the client.

Specifically, when the audit team visits a mill in rural Louisiana, they consider how they will be perceived by the general manager and plant supervisor. Both are older men with engineering degrees who have been in their current positions for more than twenty years. As a result, the team includes one of the oldest auditors (a man), an engineer (also a man, but younger), and a woman with roots in the rural South.

Conversely, when the team visits a sales office in Tokyo, they take a Japanese American, a senior auditor, and a young associate with a degree in international business.

(See the Kenton Credibility Model on page 19 for a complete explanation of the dimensions of credibility.)

You can also choose from a *variety* of sources. When your communication strategy includes sending several messages to multiple audiences, you may be able to fulfill additional objectives with a clever choice of sources.

FOR EXAMPLE

Mitchell's Department Store reengineered its discount policy, offering the same benefits to every employee, regardless of rank or tenure. Communicating this change required giving bad news to managers and good news to clerks.

Two ways that the senior executives met their goal of remotivating the managers (in addition to a new bonus package) were (1) to tell the managers personally in one-on-one meetings, and (2) to allow the managers to tell their subordinate clerks about the good news.

This strategy enhanced the perceived **credibility** of the senior executives by the managers and the managers by the clerks, thus fostering an enhanced working climate.

TIMING OPTIONS: WHEN SHOULD THE MESSAGE ARRIVE?

Again, consider the needs of your audience in conjunction with your own communication goals when deciding **when to send the message**. We too often communicate at our own convenience, which may not be consistent with the convenience of our audience. Time itself is interpreted differently in other cultures, as discussed in Chapters 3–5.

Additional considerations are sequencing and spacing, particularly with multiple audiences receiving different messages. Complex messages designed for several different audiences require careful scrutiny. Decide which audience is to receive which message in what order. Also consider how much time to allow between messages. Your selection of which audience to tell first relays a strong message in itself.

FOR EXAMPLE

The board of directors of JUMP Communications decided to centralize the strategic planning and budgeting processes of the organization, but operations remained decentralized. Nine separate divisions headquartered throughout the world were run by powerful vice presidents who had been recruited and promoted for their entrepreneurial expertise.

Obviously, this news was not going to be well received, even though operations of the divisions would remain decentralized. A hasty decision about the **timing of the message** (for example, selecting one vice president to know before others, or releasing information without evaluating potential repercussions) could sabotage the positive intention of the change.

At the suggestion of a corporate communication consultant, JUMP simultaneously faxed a *draft* of the proposal to all nine vice presidents and scheduled a meeting with the entire group to design the final plan. Equal communication eliciting equal input resulted in equal acceptance, and the change was successfully implemented.

In summary, choices of media, source, and timing can present a complex matrix of decisions. When in doubt, refer to your analysis of audience, situation, and objectives (Appendix B). What your audience wants and, secondarily, what you need are key components to decisions about communication options.

FOR EXAMPLE

When BellSouth implemented additional force reductions in 1995, careful analysis of their complex **audience, situation, and objective matrix** resulted in this communication strategy, from the perspective of a line manager in the field:

On the morning of the announcement, the president met with senior managers across the nine-state region via video teleconference. The officers of the company were on-site throughout the region to help deliver the information. Managers equipped with leader's guides returned to their respective offices to meet face to face with their employees.

At that time, the company implemented several additional communications:

- Managers received an e-mail bulletin with a discussion leader's guide.

- All employees received an online bulletin, a special edition of the company-wide newsletter, and a message left on voice mailboxes to announce how information was being distributed.

The objectives of these communications appeared to be (1) explaining the necessity of the actions being taken and the details of the plan and (2) maintaining the goodwill of the affected employees. All in all, BellSouth communicated this program in a professional manner, following the sound principles of good corporate communications.

COLLECT AND ORGANIZE YOUR INFORMATION

Too many of us try to start our preparation by collecting and organizing our information. We try to avoid the requisite first two steps in the model. Since communication is at least 50 percent common sense, you may be able to get by with a lack of analysis some of the time. However, in our current business environment, "getting by" does not provide you with a competitive advantage.

After you have considered the environment and chosen your options and are comfortable with your decisions to this point, select an appropriate organizational plan for the information for your speech, letter, interview, report, or meeting. Appendix D presents basic, flexible organizational plans; some general guidelines follow:

1. **Consider culture-specific and gender-specific information.** Review your analysis carefully to select the most persuasive information for your audiences, based on their expectations and backgrounds.

2. **Plan a beginning, a middle, and an end.** A roadmap of "tell them what you're going to tell them, then tell them, then tell them what you told them" really works. The purpose is to reinforce, not to be redundant. The consistent message ensures that you will follow through on the purpose of your communication.

FOR EXAMPLE

The Wall Street Journal reported on June 2, 1995:

> French investors are being encouraged by what they've been hearing from France's telecommunications regulator, The Direction Generale des Postes et Telecommunications, headed by Bruno Lasserre.

Mr. Lasserre said France must develop a clear **roadmap** for telecommunications competition as a way of encouraging national firms to invest in the sector.

This **roadmap**, the "tell them what you're going to tell them" of Lasserre's communication strategy, will inform his audience what to expect, which will ensure that Lasserre will follow though on his plans.

---

3. **Limit your information.** Cognitive psychologists tell us that we can easily remember between three and seven items. Busy businesspeople might remember only three. If you give them too many reasons to buy your product or implement your idea, they may remember only a few of them, and those may not be your most persuasive points.

4. **Restrict your agenda to one issue.** Select information that focuses on one specific situation or problem. Avoid wandering off to discuss other items that may be on your personal agenda but not relevant to your stated purpose.

For Example

Columnist Tom Baxter, in an essay about Newt Gingrich's communication style, wrote (lampooning Gingrich's style):

> Usually it's the last thing at the end of a long sentence that he ends up having to apologize for, such as the other day when he started answering a question about Sen. Patrick Moynihan's criticism of the GOP welfare program and ended up talking about how there is "an extraordinarily expensive government in the city of New York, absurd union work rules, and a culture of waste for which they want us to send a check." (*Atlanta Journal and Constitution*, September 21, 1995)

5. **Enhance with visual aids, numbers, and examples.** No matter how brilliantly you speak or write, your audience will remember your points better when they are supported with pictures and stories. (We believe, for example, that you will remember the information in our For Example boxes more than the facts they illustrate.) As the last step in your preparation, refer to Appendix F for important guidelines for visual aids.

For Example

A general manager at Nordstrom values **storytelling** as a management tool:

> Every morning in Africa, a gazelle wakes up knowing that it must outrun the fastest lion or be killed. Every morning in Africa, a lion wakes up knowing that it must run faster than the slowest gazelle or starve. So it doesn't really matter if you are the lion or the gazelle; when the sun comes up, start running.

Nancy K. Austin, co-author of *A Passion for Excellence*, says, "Sure, she could say something like, 'Complacency is the enemy of success,' but prowling lions and leaping gazelles turn a yawny business lesson into a life-or-death struggle." (*Working Woman*, September 1995)

6. **Tailor your message for each individual audience.** No two audiences are exactly alike, and canned material will diminish your credibility faster than anything else, except not doing your homework in the first place.

CrossTalk YOUR MESSAGE, ORAL OR WRITTEN

Now that you are armed with well-selected, organized, and supported information, you may confidently present that information by means of your chosen medium to your target audience.

ORAL MESSAGES

If you are talking to your audience (an individual or a group), follow these guidelines:

1. **Take time to warm up.** You would never consider running a race without stretching and warming up your leg muscles; you should not expect your voice and face and body to perform well if you have not worked them a little. You do not have to use formal vocal exercises; just sing in the shower or read road signs out loud on the way to work. Smiling and yawning get your facial muscles moving.

2. **Use appropriate eye contact.** "Appropriate" varies with cultural expectations (see specific chapters), but it is one of your most important considerations. Be sure to look at your entire audience, not just the decision maker.

3. **Talk *to* your audience**, not *at* them. Avoid reading unless you use a direct quotation or legal liability requires absolute accuracy. Do not memorize, either, with the possible exception of your attention-getter and final statement. You may think you can be spontaneous, but you will probably sound like a recorded message.

4. **Reduce physical barriers**, such as distance, lecterns, and stationary microphones. Many speakers stand too far from their audience behind large lecterns with attached microphones. Many interviewers position themselves across large desks. Instead, you should make every effort to show as much of yourself and get as close as is appropriate to your audience. (See specific chapters for cultural variables.)

5. **Move naturally.** Stand or sit up straight. Gesture as you do in normal conversation (your gestures may be larger if you are in front of a large audience in a large room). Stand still (most of the time), and then walk (for emphasis, transition, or variety). If you are standing, keep your weight on both feet. However, always consider the expectations of an audience with a cultural background different from your own. (See specific chapters.)

6. **Concentrate on your *audience***, not on *yourself.* Watch your audience for signs of either agreement or disagreement. Look for willingness to participate or eagerness to ask questions, and respond to the needs of your audience. However, learn to filter out irrelevant distractions, such as someone coughing or a door creaking. An audience is likely to lose interest in a speaker who appears to be focusing on his or her performance rather than on their understanding of the message. Again, be aware of cultural differences in nonverbal audience feedback.

7. **Show your audience that you care.** Nonverbal messages carry more than 65 percent of your meaning. Your audience may forgive less than perfect platform skills, but *no one* will forgive you if you do not show sincere commitment to your message and the communication of that message to your audience.

8. **Be yourself.** Most people are comfortable one-to-one but believe that they have to become someone different when they address a group. You must adapt the volume of your voice, the size of your gestures, and the extent of your movement, but whatever makes you effective one-to-one will also apply to the louder or larger you.

WRITTEN MESSAGES

If you are writing to your audience, follow these guidelines:

1. **Use the Outline Worksheet (Appendix C).** After analyzing your reader's concerns, write the most difficult sentences first. These could include initial, final, or bad news sentences. For example, in a bad news letter, you might write, "We regret that we will be unable to provide additional noncontracted consulting hours for the Ohondo-Ariato project." Using the Outline Worksheet frees you to concentrate on how best to prepare the reader for the bad news.

2. **Write as naturally as you speak.** Choose simple language and plain words.

FOR EXAMPLE

Avoid unnecessary obfuscation (confusion), such as the following:
- fiscal underachievers (poor people)
- difficult exercises in labor relations (strikes)
- satorically challenged (sloppy dressers)
- negative patient care outcome (death)
- aerodynamic personnel decelerator (parachute)
- involuntary conversion of a 747 (plane crash)

---

3. **Use active verbs whenever possible.** Using the passive voice weakens your writing. Rather than "The third-quarter report was sent last Thursday," write "We sent the third-quarter report last Thursday."

4. **Avoid slang and jargon.** Strive to write clearly by avoiding slang, jargon, acronyms, idioms, and most abbreviations. Particularly consider which expressions will not translate literally and would therefore confuse a receiver whose primary language is different from your own.

5. **Keep your sentences and paragraphs short.** In reading a sentence aloud, if you have to take a breath before the end, you will know your sentence is too long. Edit to make two sentences.

FOR EXAMPLE

Poor writers tend to use endless, revolving sentences, such as: "All committees should fully implement a by-exception style of delegation by approving the delegation of all functions to the relevant chief officer subject to specific matters being reserved for decision by the relevant member level forum."

We think this means that there is an exception to every rule. More or less.

Further, nothing discourages your reader more than long paragraphs. Avoid them. In business communication, a **one-sentence paragraph** draws attention to the information it holds. Use this technique when you want to emphasize a deadline or significant achievement.

6. **Use a single page** for most business communication such as letters, memos, and electronic mail. If a longer message is necessary (for example, a report), include an executive summary.

7. **Read aloud.** Mistakes such as word omissions, faulty subject–verb agreement, and poor logic will appear when you read aloud. If you cannot read aloud without disturbing others, simply imagine yourself reading aloud to "hear" your language.

8. **Proofread carefully.** Using your computer's spell-check feature will never substitute for a careful reading. Pay attention to recommendations from your software's grammar or style-check feature. Whenever possible, have a colleague read over an important letter or report to help spot potential problems or errors.

A WORD ABOUT INCLUSIVE LANGUAGE

Language changes as changes in society occur. For example, *idiot* and *crippled* once were acceptable clinical terms, but now we use other terms such as *developmentally disabled* or *physically challenged*.

Today, two common business communication mistakes continue to be the use of the word *he* as a generic pronoun and the word *man* as a generic term meaning human being. Proponents of this exclusive (meaning "to exclude") language argue that inclusive language is awkward and that "everyone knows what we mean."

However, consistent use of *he, him*, and *man* to refer to someone who may be male or female may limit our thinking or, worse, represent a false reality. The image that the mind creates when referring to a "he" is male, thus excluding the potential of a woman in that position or situation.

Although changes in writing and speaking habits require time and attention, the result is a message that is clearer and more precise. (See Appendix K for guidelines for inclusive language.)

FOR EXAMPLE

An article in a respected business newspaper read:
"The physician must always be educating *himself....*"
Readers might therefore presume that all physicians are men or that only male physicians need continuing education. To be more clear and precise, the columnist might have written: "Physicians must always be educating themselves."
In addition, this was overheard at a faculty meeting at a major university business school:
"We can't compare our Executive Education program to theirs; they have more *manpower* than we do."
Response from another faculty member: "Even without *female* faculty members teaching in the program?"

CONFIRM EVALUATION FOR SUCCESS

Feedback

Effective communication is an ongoing process of practice and improvement. The improvement is based on evaluating feedback from your target audiences and trusted colleagues. In addition, learn to assess accurately when your communication is "working" and when it is not, so that you can modify the areas that are less effective.

Follow these guidelines to facilitate personal improvement when you solicit and evaluate feedback:

1. **Listen carefully to comments.** We all have natural tendencies to want to defend ourselves against criticism, but it is important to hear *everything* you are told.

2. **Take notes in detail.** Write down both positives and negatives, noting questions and disagreements.

3. **Ask for specific information.** Ask for examples, and try the phrase "Please tell me more." (This is a tough one—you may not want "more" unless it's positive.) Use the reflective technique to gain more information, for example, "This is what I hear you saying...."

4. **Paraphrase to confirm meaning.** Your perceptions may not be consistent with your evaluator's intentions. For example, "You are going too fast for me" could refer to the logic in your argument or the rate of your speech.

5. **Notice nonverbal messages.** For example, the person leaning forward is probably more receptive to your message than the person leaning back.

FOR EXAMPLE

USA Today (June 19,1995) reported that the **body language** was more interesting than the rhetoric at the G7 Conference of leaders of the seven major industrial nations in Halifax, Nova Scotia.
Reporters Bill Montague and Steve Komarow described President Clinton as "thrusting his chest out in toughness." Russian President Yeltsin displayed "gestures of disgust: hands in the air, then fingers down, and a scowl."

6. **Correct in the *direction* of the evaluation.** One tendency is to overreact and to correct to the extreme. A small correction in the right direction is usually both more appropriate and more feasible. For example, feedback such as "this makes no sense at all" probably means that your argument needed more support or your transitions did not connect your ideas. Look for ways to make more "sense" rather than starting over or quitting altogether.

7. **Accept responsibility.** Another tendency is to offer reasons, justification, or apologies for any actions that generate negative feedback. No one really wants to hear those excuses, especially after being asked to give an evaluation, and no excuse facilitates improvement. Remember, you do not have to accept all feedback as equally valuable, but you are responsible for separating the useful from the useless. The ultimate accountability for your oral or written communication is, after all, yours.

8. **Recognize that your audience's perceptions define reality.** The final tendency is to reject comments with which you disagree. However, there is some truth in practically everything. Try to find that truth, and learn from the knowledge it offers.

9. **Say "thank you."** Giving feedback can be as stressful as receiving it. Positively reinforcing your evaluator will facilitate the future flow of information.

FOR EXAMPLE

Financial planner Charles Gilbert is an executive M.B.A. student at a major university. As part of his Corporate Communications course, he gave a sales presentation to his classmates. Gilbert asked his classmates to assume the role of medical residents and evaluate his presentation from that perspective. (He was preparing to give the same presentation to a group of real residents later.)

Despite Gilbert's careful preparation, the class raised several major issues and questioned him unmercifully about his choice of material.

The professor, concerned that Gilbert would be discouraged by the negative feedback, contacted him to discuss the most salient points and to bolster his confidence before his actual presentation to the medical residents. She discovered that Gilbert had followed the guidelines for evaluating feedback in the following ways:

- He listened carefully to both positive and negative comments.
- He sought additional information from the people who raised issues.
- He was open-minded about criticism and appreciative of detailed feedback.

In addition, Gilbert recognized that his practice audience shared many characteristics of his target audience, which made their comments even more relevant.

Because of his positive attitude toward **feedback** from his classmates, Gilbert received several requests from them for information about his financial planning services. Needless to say, his presentation to his "real" audience of medical residents was a major success.

Refer to Appendix H (Presentation Evaluation Form) and Appendix J (Writing Evaluation Form) for summaries of criteria for effective business speaking and writing. Your colleagues and practice audiences can use these forms to give you specific feedback. Remember to follow all the guidelines for evaluating the feedback you receive.

CREDIBILITY

The most important goal of your communication strategy is, of course, credibility. If your audience perceives that you are credible, you will be persuasive. And if you are persuasive, you will get what you want: You will achieve the objectives of your communication.

The following pragmatic model of credibility is based on the assumption that the only reality is perception. Therefore, each dimension is defined by the audience's perception of the sender's characteristics.

KENTON CREDIBILITY MODEL

- **Goodwill:** the audience's perception of your focus on and concern for them
- **Expertise:** the audience's perception of your education, knowledge, and experience
- **Power:** the audience's perception of your status, prestige, and success
- **Self-presentation:** the audience's perception of your communication skills and confidence

---

An individual's status, prestige, and success may be perceived differently depending on the specific culture of an organization or industry. However, power is even more nebulous to define. We can therefore expand the definition of power to include personal power (ability to control your own environment), interpersonal power (ability to influence other people), and corporate power (ability to mobilize resources).

IN CONCLUSION

Now for the best part:

You will achieve the perception of **goodwill** from carefully selected information based on your analysis of your audience, situation, and objectives.

You will achieve the perception of **expertise** through examples that demonstrate your knowledge, education, and experience.

You will achieve the perception of **power** with material that refers to your rank and illustrates your successes.

You will achieve the perception of effective **self-presentation** through excellent communication skills and confidence as you demonstrate those skills.

FOR EXAMPLE

On September 17, 1991, New York City experienced a disruption in telephone service that affected millions of AT&T customers and stranded thousands of airline passengers. Recognizing that the credibility of AT&T was in jeopardy, Chairman Robert E. Allen addressed the concerns of his target audiences in a full-page ad in *The New York Times* on September 23. Notice how the following excerpts illustrate the **Kenton Credibility Model**:

To establish his concern (goodwill): "I am deeply concerned...I apologize to all of you who were affected."

To confirm AT&T's experience (expertise): "No communications systems have more backup or alternative routing."

To defend AT&T's success (power): "We have designed and built our systems to the world's highest standards."

To express confidence (self-presentation): "I have great confidence in AT&T people. They have always set us apart from the competition and been the cornerstone of our customers' trust in us."

After assessing how Allen and AT&T handled the outage crisis, Todd Spinello, General Manager of Internal Billing, addressed these comments to his CEO:

> You took total ownership of the situation, admitted that management was at fault, and explained how this would not happen again. As the world's most prevalent provider of communication tools, AT&T continues to impress me with its level of commitment to process improvement and crisis management.

In summary, when planning to communicate, make sure that you:

- understand your audience, your situation, and your objectives
- consider your media, source, and timing options
- select and organize material based on that analysis

As a result, your presentation, oral or written, will be focused and confident, you will be perceived as credible and therefore persuasive, and you will increase your effectiveness as a communicator.

Suggested Readings on Business and Management Communication:

Ailes, R., with Kraushar, J. *You Are the Message.* Homewood, IL: Dow Jones-Irwin, 1988.

Barton, L. *Crisis in Organizations: Managing and Communicating in the Heat of Chaos.* Cincinnati, OH: South-Western, 1993.

Hamlin, S. *How To Talk So People Listen.* New York: Harper & Row, 1988.

Munter, M. *Guide to Managerial Communication,* 3rd ed. Englewood Cliffs, NJ: Prentice Hall, 1992.

Timm, P. R., and Stead, J. A. *Communication Skills for Business and Professions.* Englewood Cliffs, NJ: Prentice Hall, 1996.

CHAPTER 2

WHAT IF YOUR AUDIENCE IS A MAN OR A WOMAN WITH ROOTS IN THE EUROPEAN CULTURE?

Both males and females need to be aware that male dominance and female submission have been a traditional, relational pattern fostered by decades of sex-role socialization. Both sexes have become victims of rigid sex-role expectations.

CYNTHIA BERRYMAN-FINK, PH.D.

Our application of the **CrossTalk** Model begins with the largest cultural group in the American workforce: individuals who trace their roots to a European culture. In addition, our discussion will include information about individual European cultures that demonstrate some qualities unique to their EuroAmerican counterparts. (Look for the Intracultural Note icon ◐ that indicates an intracultural note.)

However, this group is extraordinarily large and complex, which complicates our attempts to offer succinct guidelines based on cultural generalities. Therefore, we are dividing this group into two cultures: men and women.

Scientists, cultural anthropologists, social psychologists, and other researchers agree that the perceptions and realities of men and women constitute separate cultural awarenesses. When these different cultural awarenesses manifest themselves in workplace communication, we find two resulting behaviors:

1. Men and women communicate *differently*.
2. Men and women communicate the same way but are *perceived differently* by audiences of both genders.

Research on gender differences in workplace communication predominantly includes American men and women with European backgrounds. However, we have excluded three types of gender research:

1. Studies of senior executives—less than 3 percent of whom are women—that conclude that no differences exist
2. Studies of freshman and sophomore college students in controlled environments
3. Studies of intimate relationships

The first is unrealistic for the overwhelming majority of the workplace population; the second and third have little relevance to the corporate environment.

As you read this chapter, remember that we have based our applications on research on American men and women with roots in European cultures. Although many of the principles apply to men and women with African, Asian, or Latino backgrounds, refer to the Genter Notes (see ☯) in those individual chapters for information focusing specifically on that culture.

Keep in mind that everything we say is based on *tendencies* of men and women as cultural groups. Individuals may exhibit any combination of male or female behaviors. In addition, many successful professionals have adopted situation-specific communication behaviors that we normally attribute to the opposite gender. We have designed suggestions and options for guidance rather than as absolute, definitive solutions.

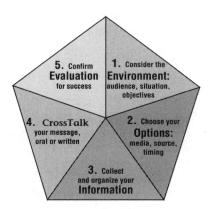

CONSIDER THE ENVIRONMENT

The environment of your communication includes the target audience, the existing situation, and your desired objectives. Your thorough understanding of all three always begins your communication process, regardless of the cultural background of your audience. However, the unique differences of your male or female target audience may determine how you analyze your situation and your objectives, so we will begin the application of the **CrossTalk** Model with audience analysis.

ANALYZE YOUR AUDIENCE

Individual traits and behaviors vary greatly. As you identify your potential audiences and learn specific details about them, use the Audience Analysis Worksheet (Appendix B) to facilitate a thorough examination of each to help avoid assumptions and the resulting miscommunication.

Identify all potential audiences: primary, hidden, and decision makers.   As we explained in Chapter 1, these can overlap, and there may be no hidden audience at all. (See Chapter 1, pages 1–21, for further explanation and example.)

Investigate and learn about each audience.   Be very careful to look beyond the obvious as you focus on **facts, attitudes, wants, and concerns**.

Facts.   Researchers have identified hundreds of facts about potential differences between the male and female individuals who may comprise your multiple audiences. We focus on the information that affects communication.
    If your receiver is a man:

- He has been socialized to perform aggressively and to boast of his successes.
- His childhood games taught him that competition is fun and winning is good. He continues to be motivated by competition.

FOR EXAMPLE

Herbert M. Baum, President of Quaker State Corporation, reflected on his success at Campbell Soup Company, where he helped build the Prego brand: "I'm obsessed with **winning** more than I am with making a lot of money." (*The Wall Street Journal*, July 14, 1995)

- He views conflict as impersonal, a necessary part of working relationships.
- He has traditionally been afforded attention-getting roles, as reflected in his interest in personal benefit and use of the word *I*.
- He is impressed by power, ability, and achievement.

- His left-brain orientation yields problem-solving skills that are logical, analytical, factual, and hierarchical.
- He tends to focus on one thing at a time.
- His friendships are built on mutual activities and goals. He builds trust on the basis of actions and accomplishments.
- He may hear only your literal words and miss your underlying emotion. He is not likely to express his true feelings through facial expressions.
- His communication style tends to be direct.
- When he succeeds, he attributes it to his ability. When he fails, he attributes the failure to outside circumstances, or he blames someone else.

If your receiver is a woman:

- She has been socialized to work cooperatively and to be modest about her successes.
- Her childhood games taught her to compromise and collaborate, and she continues to be motivated by affiliation. She competes primarily with herself, that is, with her own expectations of what she should be able to accomplish.
- She takes conflict personally.

Women with roots in eastern European Jewish, Italian, and Greek cultures, however, tend to view **conflict** as a positive function of a close relationship.

- She has traditionally been afforded attention-giving roles, as reflected in her interest in the wider needs of the corporate community and use of the word *we*.
- She is impressed by personal disclosure and professional courage.
- Her right-brain orientation yields problem-solving skills that are creative, sensitive, and nonhierarchical.
- She has the ability to focus on multiple projects simultaneously. She is probably accustomed to balancing the demands of work, family, home, school, or community issues and thus applies these skills to her job.
- Her friendships are based on personal closeness. She builds trust by sharing both her secrets and herself.
- She may be proficient at decoding your nonverbal meanings and is likely to display her feelings through facial expression or body language.
- Her style will tend to be indirect, except with other women of equal rank.

- When she succeeds, she may believe she was lucky. When she fails, she blames herself.

Attitudes.   The gender of both the sender and the receiver affects your audience's attitudes about you, about your topic, and about being there to receive your information.

First, consider your receivers' **attitudes about you**.

If you are communicating:

- Man to man, he may afford you instant credibility based on similarity.
- Man to either man or woman, you may begin with a higher perception of credibility than your female counterpart has, especially in terms of expertise, status, and power.
- Man to woman, she may expect that you will not really listen to her. She may also surmise that your idea or plan is based on your independent thinking and that it is an inflexible decision with little opportunity for compromise.
- Woman to woman, she may expect you to be friendly, nurturing, and concerned. She may afford you instant credibility based on similarity.
- Woman to either man or woman, you should expect to have to demonstrate better skills and more experience than your male counterpart does to be perceived as equal to him in credibility.
- Woman to man, there are two major issues to consider:

    1. He will expect you to be friendly and nurturing, even passive-dependent. Any aggressive behavior or other deviation from his expectations can cause discomfort, confusion, or negative responses.

FOR EXAMPLE

The CEO of an international corporation addressed the graduating class at a major women's college. Included in his inspirational speech about the changing workplace and resulting opportunities for women were these revealing comments:

> I represent America's senior corporate leadership today: I am sixty-two years old. I have an undergraduate engineering degree and was a military officer in Korea. As with most men my age, neither my grandmothers nor my mother nor my wife ever worked outside the home. I spent the first twenty-five years of my business career competing in an all-male business world.
>
> Men my age relate well to their daughters, daughters-in-law, and women in the workplace in general—and we learn a lot from them. But we just don't have the background or the experience to relate to these changes *comfortably* and with *confidence*.

His response is classic: **discomfort** and **confusion** resulting in a **negative response**.

2. He may simply disregard you.

Mary Rudie Barneby, President of Regis Retirement Plan Services Inc., a pension plan subsidiary of United Asset Management, who has been cited as one of America's fifty most powerful women managers, described her sense of being **disregarded**:
    "It isn't a glass ceiling," she says, that prevents women from reaching the top; instead, she envisions a room divided by a one-way mirror, with the male executives all on one side, talking among themselves and competing with each other.
    "We can see them, but they can't see us," she observes. (*The Wall Street Journal*, July 26, 1995)

Men and women with roots in the European culture may have different initial reactions to and **attitudes about your topic**. Your female audience members' greater psychological resilience makes them more agreeable to change, which is, of course, an element in most persuasive messages. Your male receivers may accept your message only if they immediately perceive personal benefit.

Finally, men and women may respond differently to actually being your audience. That is, they may have different **attitudes about being there** to receive your memo, hear your presentation, or attend your meeting.

Your male receiver is more likely to be an autocratic problem solver. He may resent interrupting his schedule to hear your message, unless the other audience members are hierarchically superior, and thus inclusion is a compliment. He will assume that your presentation of a problem is a direct request for a solution.

Your female receiver, often a team player who is motivated by acceptance and affiliation, is more likely to appreciate being included in your audience. She will listen carefully and respond to your presentation of a problem with support and reassurance, and she will offer to share experiences and jointly discuss the solution.

The Clarence Thomas confirmation hearings almost came to a dead stop when Anita Hill's female friend was questioned by the Senate committee. Members of the committee, all male, were incredulous that her friend had not told Hill what to do when Hill told her about the alleged harassment.
    In reality, Hill's friend was responding in a gender-specific manner. When Hill reported the alleged sexual harassment, her friend **listened** and **commiserated**, but she did not offer a solution.

In analyzing attitudes, remember that your audience may prefer to be somewhere else, doing something else, with someone else. However, it is likely that the women to whom you write and speak will be more receptive to you, your topic, and being there than a male counterpart.

The stereotypical image of the "ugly American" derives from the perception that Americans are aggressive, self-centered, and expect everything to be done their way and in their language. People in other countries and from other cultures often describe their U.S. colleagues and clients as loud, rude, and overpersonal.

Recognize that your audience might share these perceptions about **you, your topic,** and **being there** to receive your message. Plan strategies to establish a more accurate understanding of you and your intentions.

Wants.   The next step in audience analysis involves your determination of what information your audience wants to know. Avoid confusing what they want to know with what you believe they "need to know." Until you tell them what they *want* to know, they may not be receptive to what they *need* to know.

A man is likely to **want to know** the benefit for himself and just what he has to do to win. He may be thinking, "What's in this for me?" and "What's the bottom line?" He will want to know how your plan will help him compete, both as an individual and as an organization.

FOR EXAMPLE

When William Larian, Research and Development Manager for SAFE Foods, finally was summoned to the chairman's office to describe a new process for freezing produce, he came prepared with reams of documentation, all of which he wanted to present.

In less than ten minutes of recitation, the chairman bellowed: "Get to the point! What's the bottom line? Can we beat the competition? How much will it cost?"

The next time (though he didn't think there would be a next time), Larian vowed to give the chairman just what he **wanted to know**. He would present his conclusions with brief support and specific benefits. He would offer detail only when asked or in written documentation.

A woman is likely to **want to know** the benefit for the individuals in the organization and what she should do to facilitate the process. She may be thinking, "What will be the impact of this plan on the working relationships of the people involved?" She will want to know how your "winning" plan will allow her to provide a win–win situation for everyone rather than a loss for someone.

Germans tend to be conservative and disciplined. They will **want to know,** for example, how your proposal meets their criteria for logical process or carefully structured change.

Concerns. Finally, your audiences' fears—the **consistent concerns** that your male and female audience members express—often present a summary of their individual gender differences.

Again, a caveat: *Do not assume* that every man and woman will exhibit each gender-specific trait. In fact, many men and women have adopted situation-specific, successful behavior of the opposite gender.

You may expect, however, that a careful review of these traits will enhance the depth of your understanding about your audience and therefore increase the probability that you will select the appropriate persuasive information.

Remember:

- Men tend to be most concerned about winning. They will work as hard as necessary to win against their standard of comparison, usually other men. They fear defeat. They are interested in how facts affect the bottom line.
- Women tend to be most concerned with relationships. They work to do their best; their standard of comparison is their personal ideal of their own abilities. They fear that their successes mean someone else's defeat. They are interested in how the process affects the organization as a whole.

Analyzing your audience may be the most important component of your entire communication process, because every decision you make depends on your accuracy and detail at this point. In summary:

1. Identify your primary, hidden, and decision-making audiences.
2. Discover personal and professional facts, avoiding generalizations.
3. Be aware of their attitudes about you, your subject, and being there to receive your message.
4. Determine what they *want* to know, over and above what they *need* to know.
5. Recognize consistent concerns.

ANALYZE YOUR SITUATION

Identify and define the problem.   Isolate the decision that now requires you to communicate a message to a particular audience.

1. What is the distinct cause for the message you are preparing?
2. What are the specific parameters that reduce the situation to manageable proportions?

Both your gender and that of your audience can affect the definition of the problem. A man may define a problem in terms of outcome. A woman may define the same problem in terms of the people affected. Be certain that your definition of the problem is consistent with that of your male or female receiver and that you anticipate a mixed audience of both men and women.

FOR EXAMPLE

When Shan Carr's new manager asked her to write an evaluation of her department for him, her initial response was to appraise the performance of her subordinates in terms of teamwork and client relationships. However, after careful consideration of how her new male boss might assess the situation, she added detailed information about what her people actually did and what they accomplished as a result of their efforts.

On the other hand, when Bill Tucker's new female manager asked him for the same information about his department, Bill described his group as "winners" and offered facts and figures to support his assessment. She was impressed with his confidence and his report, but she was concerned that the competitive spirit that Bill described might create dissension within his team.

Evaluate the corporate culture surrounding the problem.   A woman may be more sensitive to the nebulous attitudes and norms shared by members of an organization, even though men probably established that behavior. Therefore, a female audience member will recognize if your plan or idea or even a potential employee's behavior is consistent with that of the corporate culture. Male audience members, though acutely recognizing the presence or absence of "fit," may not attribute the reason to the effects of culture.

Despite their sensitivity to culture, however, women may not be as involved in office politics, which reduces their comprehensive understanding of the *overall* culture.

Corporate culture begins at the top of the organizational ranks; therefore, these figures are particularly meaningful:

- Men comprise 90.5 percent of the membership on corporate boards in the United States. (*Atlanta Journal and Constitution*, July 28, 1995)
- Men comprise 90 percent of the membership on corporate boards in Canada. (*Women in Management*, September–October, 1995)
- Although there are 600 women on Fortune 500 boards in the United States, there are no female CEOs. (*USA Today*, October 10, 1995)
- Women own 37 percent of U.S. businesses, which generate $1.4 trillion in sales and employ 15.5 million people (35 percent more than all Fortune 500 firms). (*Atlanta Journal and Constitution*, October 15, 1995)

Assess the external climate.   If you or your audience is male, you tend to focus more on what is going on in the specific industry and in related industries than do your female colleagues, who may focus more specifically on internal issues.

FOR EXAMPLE

Jack Hunter and Connie Fisher were at odds over selecting an advertising agency to handle their new product. Hunter wanted to eliminate one agency because the ad team just didn't "fit" with the organization. Fisher voted against the other agency because their campaign was inconsistent with the work ethic displayed by the CEO. Though offering different perspectives, both Hunter and Fisher were expressing concerns over **corporate culture**.

Hunter and Fisher's controversy continued as they reviewed the work of two additional agencies. Hunter liked the third agency because their campaign reflected the industry norm (**external climate**). Fisher liked the fourth agency because their campaign coincided with the emotional expression of the people in the organization.

They finally agreed on an entirely different agency. Hunter liked it because the agency representatives looked and talked like members of his own organization, yet the campaign was innovative within the industry. Fisher believed that the commercials and prints ads accurately represented the emotional concepts of the organization.

ANALYZE YOUR OBJECTIVES

Most messages, no matter how simple or apparently insignificant, encompass **three objectives: an overall goal, a specific purpose of the communication, and a hidden agenda**.

The **overall goal**, based on the mission statement of the organization, should be inherent in any corporate message and may appear to be a guideline for all your objectives. However, if you are a man, you may take the actual words of the mission statement literally, whereas your female counterpart may broadly apply the intention and allow for a more liberal interpretation.

The **specific purpose of the communication** depends on your needs and on your analysis of the target audience. Also consider your own gender tendencies. Men tend to overestimate their potential for success, whereas women tend to underestimate. As you assess your audience's level of knowledge about your topic, realize that your male audiences may allege more knowledge than they actually have, whereas your female audiences may be modest about their knowledge.

FOR EXAMPLE

Sam Polk and Mildred Johansen were each preparing budget requests for their departments. They knew that the average increases were expected to be about 8 percent. Objectively, their past achievements and future need projections were equal, and the budget committee's preplanning had assessed their potential increases at about 7 percent each.

Polk reasoned that if 8 percent was average, someone was going to get more, and it might as well be him. So he **overestimated** his budget and asked for 12 percent. Johansen reasoned that she could manage with as little as 6 percent and humbly **underestimated** her budget to that amount. She assumed that if more money were available, she would receive it, based on her achievements.

The budget committee awarded Polk a 10 percent increase and Johansen a 6 percent increase, thus meeting their 8 percent average.

Polk received the additional money not because he deserved it more than Johansen did, but because *he asked for it.*

And finally, you have a **hidden agenda**, a personal objective to which you are aspiring. *Everybody* has one, including the members of your audience. Men's goals are likely to be competitive; women's goals may be affiliative. Men may even interrupt when they notice chances to offer information that fulfills their hidden agendas. Women may be more indirect and wait for an opening.

CHOOSE YOUR OPTIONS

After evaluating your audience, situation, and objectives, you can explore the communication **options** available to you: how the message should be sent (**medium**), who should send it (**source**), and when it should arrive (**timing**).

MEDIA OPTIONS: HOW SHOULD THE MESSAGE BE SENT?

As you assess your options for **how your message should be sent** to your intended receiver, review Table 1.1 (page 19). Remember that your media choices should be based on the wants and needs of your target audience, rather than on your own. Here are some additional considerations:

Your male receiver may:

- Never hear a message circulating on the **grapevine**, particularly if there are women in this communication network.

Your female receiver may:

- Receive your message from the **grapevine** quicker than you want her to, particularly if other women are in the communication network. (Depending on the number of people who repeated the message on its way to her, what she hears may be distorted.)

- Expect to discuss important information with you in a casual **conversation**, especially if you are a man.
- Be defensive about being called to a formal **interview**, especially if you are a woman.

- Be annoyed by a **phone call** that interrupts him, particularly if the caller is a subordinate who does not make the benefit clear.
- Pay little attention in a **meeting or formal presentation**, unless he understands immediate personal benefit and recognizes that his superiors are included as well.

- Appreciate the technology involved in a **teleconference**.

- Access his **electronic mail** often and enthusiastically, especially if he is younger.
- Not recognize the personal energy involved in a **personal note**.

- Prefer the brevity of a **memo**.

- Appreciate a **letter** that he can read at a time of his own choosing.
- Read only the executive summary and selected sections of a **report**.
- Be impressed by your title on your **business card**.

- Appreciate information received in informal **conversation**.

- Be intimidated by a formal **interview**, especially if she is a subordinate who is "summoned" to your office. She may expect that your purpose is negative, that is, that she has done something wrong.
- Sound hesitant in response to your **phone call** that caught her off guard or unprepared.

- Appreciate being included in a problem-solving **meeting**, and offer her attention and positive nonverbal feedback to your **formal presentation**. Do not overestimate her approval, however.
- Appear uncomfortable in a **teleconference** where nonverbal behaviors are altered by technology.
- Access her **electronic mail** seldom and tentatively, particularly if she is older.
- Appreciate the thought and effort that went into a **personal note or a greeting card** that recognizes a special occasion.
- Feel short-changed by the brevity or terseness of a **memo**.
- Try to read the hidden meaning in a **letter**.
- Be impressed by the detail you include in a **report**.
- Recognize the creative aspects of your **business card**.

SOURCE OPTIONS: WHO SHOULD DELIVER THE MESSAGE?

When selecting the **source—the person to deliver your message**—the most important criterion is the perceived credibility of that source by your target audience.

Again, remember to make this decision based on the needs of your male or female receiver rather than on your own.

Note the following mitigating gender factors:

- Both male and female audiences tend to perceive men as having more credibility than women with equal rank, experience, and training.
- Similarity is a criterion for perception of credibility. Therefore, men tend to be more credible to other men. Women may be more credible to some other women.
- As a function of similarity, male receivers are more likely than their female counterparts to require that the message be delivered from a source with *status* equal to or greater than their own. Note, as well, that a man's higher status might outweigh a woman's similarity to a female receiver.
- Some researchers contend that men are always the most credible choice to deliver the message. You should be more realistic in your viewpoints.

FOR EXAMPLE

"Women Gain Power in the Ad World," a *USA Today* cover story (June 12, 1995) reported that "women's communication skills often make them more **credible** and therefore better at massaging client relationships and consumers' emotions—the heart of advertising."

Melanie Wells suggests that recognition of women's acumen in this area has increased career path opportunities in account planning, a relatively new discipline in advertising. She quotes Gotham Chairman Stone Roberts: "Even if the old male bastion doesn't want to admit it, women are better at this business."

We suggest, as well, that you investigate your options to include ways in which other sources may be "similar" to your receiver.

FOR EXAMPLE

Jerry Fogarty, marketing vice president for an asset-based lending institution, hired Tracie Banister to make cold calls to prospective clients. A young woman with a college degree in marketing, Banister prepared thoroughly, presented impressively, and achieved a respectable average of successful calls.

Her success rate with older men, however, was almost zero. The obvious solution, based on the "similarity equals credibility" theory, was to hire an older man to call other older men.

Fogarty was unwilling to accept this biased solution and instead suggested that Banister establish rapport with the younger and often female assistants to the older men.

As a result of this strategy with a **similar** audience, Banister improved her success rate in initiating increased opportunities for the organization. (See the Kenton Credibility Model on page 19 in Chapter 1 for more information.)

The variety of opportunities that exists in choosing the source of your message is increased by your considerations of gender. When several messages are intended for multiple audiences, you may be able to meet additional objectives with a clever choice of sources.

In the United States, information tends to flow from the subordinate to the manager. In the European organization, where authority is usually centralized, information flows from the managers to the subordinates. Therefore, managers must be more assertive about seeking out information from their employees. American managers who automatically expect to be kept informed by their European subordinates might be disappointed.

Therefore, consider a private presentation to the top-ranking German executive first. That individual may choose to personally present your proposal to other decision makers on your behalf or to endorse your speech when you make it. Either option would enhance both the perception of your credibility and the potential for your success.

TIMING OPTIONS: WHEN SHOULD THE MESSAGE ARRIVE?

Again, consider the needs of your audience in conjunction with your own communication objectives when deciding **when to send the message**. We too often communicate at our own convenience, which may not be consistent with the **timing** needs of our male or female audience.

Your male receiver is more likely to be rigid about the deadline he has set for you, even though he is more relaxed about his own deadlines. Your female receiver is more likely to be considerate of your needs in adjusting a deadline, but she is probably very concerned about keeping hers.

Mistakes in decisions about the **timing** of your message could cost you the deal or the client.

For example, your French colleagues would prefer to socialize over their meals and discuss business after dinner. (Remember, however, that even social conversation does not concern personal issues. The French prefer to discuss topics such as sports, politics, or the arts.)

An American audience might allow you to "get straight to the point" (although we rarely recommend this approach).

The complex messages that you send to multiple male and female audiences require analysis that includes information about gender and about the specific individuals involved. Review your Audience Analysis Worksheet (Appendix B) for all of your audiences when you consider the order of your messages and how much time there is between them.

COLLECT AND ORGANIZE YOUR INFORMATION

If you have done your homework to this point, you have considered the environment and chosen your options. In other words, you understand your target audiences, your objectives with each of those audiences, the situation in which you are involved, and your choices in terms of media, source, and timing. Selecting the appropriate information and format will now fall into place more easily.

The organizational plans in Appendix D are flexible, depending on your specific choices. Keep the following gender qualifiers in mind, however, when applying your information to the outline models for audiences with roots in the European culture.

1. **Plan a beginning, a middle, and an end** to provide a roadmap or agenda of your message.

   For your male receivers:

   - Emphasize *personal* benefit in the introduction.
   - Be succinct with your introduction (but do not delete it), so that you can quickly make your point.
   - Reestablish personal benefit in the conclusion.

   For your female receivers:

   - Emphasize the benefits for her department or team in the introduction.
   - State the organizational plan for your presentation and stick to it.
   - Confirm a win–win situation in the conclusion.

Consider cultural implications when you plan your **agenda**.

- For example, a graphic picture of a bloody car crash would be acceptable in the United States to open a presentation about legislating speed limits. Germans, however, tend to dislike the sight of blood, and violence is likely to offend the British.
- Devote significant time and attention to the introduction phase of your communication with Europeans, whether it is written correspondence, a presentation, or a meeting. Allow them to get to know you as you build up to your proposal.

2. **Limit your information** (Remember that most communication experts recommend no more than three main points.)

   For your male receivers:

   - Be direct with your main points.
   - Include issues concerning long-term impact on the organization's bottom line.

For your female receivers:

- Consider an indirect approach to your main points.
- Include issues concerning short-term impact on individuals and teams.

3. **Enhance with visual aids, numbers, and examples.** (Appendix F contains guidelines for visual aids.)

For your male receivers:

- Illustrate your points with numbers that impact the bottom line.
- Avoid personal disclosure to illustrate professional points, especially if you are a woman.
- Avoid attempting to impress your male audience with sports metaphors, especially if don't fully understand them yourself.

FOR EXAMPLE

An otherwise articulate communications consultant is notorious for mixing sports **metaphors**: "When the ball is in your court, pick it up and run with it...." Although such a mistake may provide a humorous moment, it is not good for credibility.

For your female receivers:

- Employ personal anecdotes; they will respond to personal disclosure.
- Be careful with sports or war metaphors, especially if you are a man, unless you are certain that your audience will appreciate them.

 Your German audience will be very inquisitive and will appreciate detailed supporting evidence for your argument. Avoid humorous anecdotes in presentations and business meetings; the Germans may view them as distracting.

---

4. **Tailor your message for each individual audience.**

Remember: These are guidelines, not absolutes. You can never assume that any individual is going to think or behave a certain way simply because of gender. However, allow this information to expand your thinking and broaden your considerations as you select the most appropriate and effective material for conveying each message to each audience.

In addition, even if your European audience speaks English as a second language or you speak their language, use an interpreter for business negotiations. That way, you can focus on the nuances of the deal rather than on the problems of the language.

An audience who speaks English does not necessarily speak "American." Be especially aware that the same word can have different meanings. For example:

- In England, a billion is a million million (1,000,000,000,000); in the United States and Canada, a billion is a thousand million (1,000,000,000).
- In an American meeting, if you "table" a subject, you postpone it to a later date; in an British meeting, if you "table" a subject, you discuss it now.
- The word *gift* in English translates to "poison" in German. This is one of many examples why a translator or language consultant is vital to your presentation, negotiation, or product promotion.

CrossTalk YOUR MESSAGE, ORAL OR WRITTEN

Now that you are armed with well-selected, organized, and supported information, you may confidently present that information by means of your chosen medium to your target audience. Our term **CrossTalk** refers to the way you alter your behavior in order to communicate more effectively with individuals from different cultures.

ORAL MESSAGES

Refer to the guidelines for speaking to individuals or groups on pages 14–15 in Chapter 1. Here are some additional suggestions, based on both your gender and that of your audience with roots in the European culture.

If you are a man speaking to men:

- Express your confidence through direct eye contact, but do not expect them to reciprocate.
- Expect interruptions and appreciate them, since they indicate that your male audience is listening.
- Avoid being overenthusiastic about your topic.

FOR EXAMPLE

When Eugene's sales manager jokingly referred to his communication style as resembling Billy Bob of Billy Bob's Car Land, Eugene realized that he was perceived as **overenthusiastic**, and he worked to control his energy and tone down his presentation.

If you are a man speaking to women:

- Warm up your facial muscles to enhance your ability to express yourself through facial expression.

> Smile, yawn, and make faces on your way to the meeting or presentation—when no one can see you.

- Make direct eye contact with each individual.
- Allow enough space for your female receivers to be comfortable. Watch for signs such as stepping away or sitting back in their seats that indicate you are too close.
- Be sensitive to their subtle indications of lack of understanding or need to question. Encourage feedback during your presentation since they may be hesitant to interrupt you.
- Develop and communicate a transition from their thought to yours, rather than ignoring their comments and just changing the subject.
- Show enthusiasm for your product or idea. Your female audience may interpret a relaxed style as uncaring.

If you are a woman speaking to men:

- Warm up your voice to achieve the deepest, most well-projected sound that is possible for you. Your male audience will expect you to have excellent vocal skills.

> To find your lowest natural pitch, lie flat on your back, relax, breathe from your diaphragm without moving your shoulders, and then speak. Try to maintain that sound for a deeper, more resonant voice that will carry in a large room.

- Warm up your body so that you will be more comfortable using whatever space is available for you.

> Walk briskly around the building or stretch in the ladies' room.

- Express your confidence through direct eye contact. Do not look down or at the ceiling.
- Avoid reading or even appearing to read, which reduces the perception of your confidence and therefore your credibility.
- Remove physical barriers that diminish your size, such as lecterns. Try to stand, if your audience is sitting. If you must sit, try to use a seat that puts you at a level equal to or higher than that of your male audience.
- Employ natural, broad movements to convey confidence. Relax; a perception of nervousness will damage your credibility.
- Avoid tag questions, that is, phrases attached to statements that change the statement to a question such as "This is a great idea, don't you think?". Your male receivers may perceive that you lack confidence about your statement.

FOR EXAMPLE

A female partner at a "Big Six" accounting firm, considered by her peers as an authority on financial issues, speaks at industry meetings worldwide. When asked her secret about communicating in an environment filled with men, she replied, "Men like to hear them-*selves* talk. When *women* have something to say, it had better be powerful and to the point." (Emphasis added.)

- Anticipate interruptions as normal male communication rather than personal attacks or even negative feedback.
- Recognize that you may receive little if any active listening, such as smiles or head nodding. This does not mean they are not listening.
- Control your energy, and focus your enthusiasm. If you are too dramatic, your male audience may enjoy your performance but miss your message.

If you are a woman speaking to women:

- Warm up your facial muscles so that the smile your female audience is expecting will look natural and so that you can freely express the emotional content of your message in your facial expression.
- Reduce space barriers to a minimum by getting as close as you can to your large audience and by sitting on an equal level with an individual or small group.
- Take advantage of your female audience's tendency to be able to read the true emotional context of your message by using your face, hands, and body to express yourself.
- Understand that the active listening and nonverbal feedback you are likely to receive may be more polite than positive.
- Express your enthusiasm sincerely and personally.

Finally, be yourself. Remember that most people are comfortable one-to-one but believe that they have to become someone different when they address a group. These suggestions are designed to help you become more adaptable to multiple communication situations, not to change you into someone else (see box on page 41).

WRITTEN MESSAGES

If you are writing to your audience with roots in the European culture, consider these guidelines in addition to the ones on pages 15–16 in Chapter 1, based both on your gender and that of your audience.

Just in case **"being yourself"** includes a very casual or expressive style, here are some additional points to remember:

- Northern Europeans wait until invited to use first names. In U.S. organizations, being on a first-name basis, even with individuals who are older or senior, is typical business practice.

- In general, be cautious of hand gestures, since many gestures have different meanings in different cultures. (However, your Italian audience may consider you boring if you do not gesture expressively.) For example:

    - Germans indicate *one* by raising a thumb and *two* by raising a thumb and index finger. Therefore, if you indicate *one* by holding up your index finger, your audience may think you are indicating *two*.

    - Italians wave good-bye by raising one hand with the palm facing the body and moving the hand back and forth to and from the body.

    - British speakers keep your attention by looking away while they talk. In the United States, speakers tend to look more directly at their audiences. The French tend to maintain continual eye contact as well.

    - In the United States, relaxed posture often indicates comfort and confidence. However, your northern European audiences may be concerned about your proper upbringing if you do not sit and stand straight and tall.

    - Germans conduct business in a formal, serious, and impersonal manner; they will appreciate the same conduct from you.

    - Canadian businesspeople tend to more reserved and formal than their North American colleagues. Be direct but polite.

If you are a man writing to a man, or a woman writing to a woman:

- When writing to someone of your own gender, your task tends to be easy. Simply imagine yourself in a conversation and write accordingly.

If you are a man writing to a woman:

- Temper a direct approach with polite buffers and qualifiers.
- Emphasize the positive points. Her cognitive filter may cause her to focus on your negative messages and miss your positive messages.
- Avoid exaggeration, particularly of your own accomplishments.
- Be careful with gender-specific metaphors, especially about war or sports.

If you are a woman writing to a man:

- Avoid qualifiers, disclaimers, fillers, and intensifiers, all of which reduce the impact of your message.

FOR EXAMPLE

She wrote: "I don't know if this is right, but I believe that maybe we should consider the possibility that the conference participants might really like a break in, say, about hour intervals."

(He would have written: "Break every hour.")

She wrote: "I hope you know how really thrilled I am with your delightful presentation. I loved your fascinating stories."

(He would have written: "I am pleased with your insightful proposal.")

- Avoid excessive cushioning of negative information. His cognitive filter may cause him to focus on your positive messages and miss your negative messages.
- Curb your impulse to flaunt your vocabulary, especially if you perceive yours to be superior to his. He will not be impressed.
- Be careful with gender-specific metaphors, especially about homemaking, cooking, or childbirth.

FOR EXAMPLE

A successful but frustrated grantswriter, suppressing the urge to edit her proposal "just one more time" before sending it out, told her male boss that she was about to "stop panting and start pushing." If he had not been through childbirth classes with his wife, he might not have understood the metaphor.

Here are some additional specifics about writing to European audiences:

- In Europe or Canada, the date October 4, 1996, is written 4.10.96. In the United States, we would write 10/4/96. Individuals who did not understand this difference might unintentionally promise delivery of a product in April but plan to ship the following October.
- Germans tend to be restrained and given to understatement. As a result, they will not be impressed by exaggeration or hype. The German executive who speaks softly in a meeting is likely to be the one with the most power.
- The French tend to avoid "I" and "my," saying instead "It is said that...." Americans may perceive this passive language as avoiding responsibility; the French, however, are being polite.
- Avoid the "hard sell" approach with Canadian audiences.

CONFIRM EVALUATION FOR SUCCESS

The differences in the way men and women receive feedback tend to be so substantial and obvious that even cartoonists lampoon them.

Woman wearing tight pants, looking in the mirror: "Oh, no! I've lost control! I've eaten too much! I must have gained 20 pounds!"

Man wearing tight pants, looking in the mirror: "Oh, no! Those new cleaners shrunk my pants!"

As you seek evaluation to confirm your communication success, do *not* assume that all biases and expectations will be the same in terms of presenting and receiving oral and written communication even though

1. English is the language of international business.
2. Many Europeans' English sounds similar to that spoken in the United States.
3. The cultural roots that affect communication behavior are shared by Europeans and EuroAmericans *as a group*.

Differences regarding giving and receiving feedback center on the ways in which men and women listen, attribute success and failure, accept responsibility and blame, and filter positive and negative information.

LISTENING BEHAVIOR

In general, when a woman listens, she offers an active response; that is, she nods her head or says "um-hum" to indicate her attention. A man who is actively listening is more likely to simply look directly at the speaker without moving or speaking. A positive response from him indicates "yes," not just "I'm listening."

Listening behavior varies across cultures. For example:
- In France, both the speaker and the listener maintain eye contact.
- American listening behavior usually involves staring directly at the speaker's eyes, one and then the other, and then darting glances over the speaker's shoulders.
- British listeners tend to focus on a spot in front of the speaker, so that both eyes appear to be looking directly into the speaker's eyes.
- Germans tend to reserve their smiles for relatives and close friends.

ATTRIBUTING SUCCESS AND FAILURE

When a man succeeds, he believes that it is because of his ability. When he fails, be believes that the situation was simply beyond his control (that is, his assistant didn't prepare the correct report, the client wasn't ready to buy, or the deal wasn't meant to be). When a woman succeeds, she believes that she was lucky, had an excellent support team, or was in the right place at the right time. When she fails, she believes that she simply lacked ability.

Unfortunately, both male and female observers intensify these unbalanced perceptions. Both men and women tend to believe that a man succeeds because of his ability. Conversely, both men and women tend to believe that a woman succeeds because she works very hard and the task is easy.

FOR EXAMPLE

A female professor at a top business school began work on her Ph.D. at age thirty-five. A single mother with a child to support, she continued teaching a full load throughout her program and still managed to graduate in four years and publish part of her dissertation.

Exhausted but elated, she expected accolades from her colleagues. The most memorable comment, however, came from her male Associate Dean: "Are you already finished? Must have been a much **easier** program than the one I went through!"

ACCEPTING RESPONSIBILITY AND BLAME

Men tend to have a difficult time understanding that assuming responsibility does not mean accepting blame. Since a man does not disassociate responsibility and blame, he often refuses both. He, additionally, may allow the blame to fall on whoever is willing to accept it.

A woman is quick to say "I'm sorry," meaning that she regrets that something happened, not that she regrets she did it. However, she may find herself not only responsible, but at fault, by her own admission.

FOR EXAMPLE

A man, absorbed in a report he is reading, turns a corner and collides with a woman coming down the hall. She says, "Pardon me!" He says, "That's all right."

In a serious corporate crisis, the same man is likely to avoid any action that may be perceived as assuming **responsibility**, because he associates it with taking the **blame**. The same woman is likely to unknowingly assume responsibility and be assigned blame when she simply expresses regret that the situation occurred.

FILTERING GOOD AND BAD NEWS

Male defense mechanisms are better developed than those of women, which means that men tend to be better at shaping reality to their own advantage. As a result, men tend to focus on positive information and filter out the negative, which results in positive self-esteem but little improvement. Women, on the other hand, tend to focus on negative information and filter out the positive, which offers them greater potential for improvement but continues to challenge self-esteem.

FOR EXAMPLE

The senior partner at a prestigious law firm expressed concern about his two new attorneys.

When Thomas Wingate lost a case, he disregarded the loss without examining the reasons for it. Wingate was always eager to begin another case.

When Sarah Foley lost a case, she agonized over its every detail. Foley was reluctant to begin another case until she had learned everything she could about the one she had lost.

As a result, Wingate started his next case quickly and confidently, if not better prepared. Foley approached her next case more slowly, with more knowledge but less confidence.

Europeans often choose words that sound more final, extreme, or **negative** than the actual intended meaning. For example:

- Your German manager may declare your report wrong and unacceptable when it needs only minor editing.

- Your French clients' "no!" may mean "maybe," and they may eventually agree to your proposal. They may argue with you because they find your argument stimulating.

- Your British (or Australian) colleagues might respond to your idea by indicating that you don't know what you are talking about; they are most likely looking for a spirited argument, your participation in which will enhance your credibility.

- When Americans say "quite good," they mean "very good"; when the English say "quite good," they mean "less than good."

SOLICITING AND EVALUATING FEEDBACK

Here are some guidelines, in addition to those on pages 17–19 in Chapter 1, to facilitate your ability to solicit and evaluate feedback from your audience with roots in the European culture.

If you are a man receiving feedback:

- Avoid interrupting; this is your time to listen, not to talk.

Scandinavians tend to be particularly annoyed when Americans **interrupt** them.

- Write down negative comments with the same detail that you note positive comments.

- Ask for examples of negative comments, not just positive ones.
- Look for nonverbal messages along with literal ones.
- Avoid rejecting information with which you do not agree, recognizing that there is some truth in every perception.
- Accept responsibility. You are being held accountable, not being blamed.
- Plan some change in behavior as a result of this feedback.
- Express sincere appreciation for all the feedback, not just the *positive* part.
- Leave the evaluator with the perception that you understood all the feedback, both positive and *negative*.

FOR EXAMPLE

Nina DiSesa, Executive Vice President, McCann Erickson, New York, offered a suggestion to women who give feedback to men:
"You can't make them feel you're bossing them around. Men are more sensitive when women are in the driver's seat." (*USA Today*, June 12, 1995)

If you are a woman receiving feedback:

- Expect interruptions from the men to whom you are speaking.
- Write down positive comments with the same detail that you note negative comments.
- Ask for positive comments in writing.
- Avoid overinterpreting nonverbal information. Pay attention to the actual words, especially if the sender is a man. If the sender is a woman, her nonverbal cues are important, but they should not lead you to exaggerate their meaning.
- Avoid overreacting. Plan a minimum of correction in the direction of the evaluation. (Your minimum response will probably be perceived as a large behavioral change.)
- Avoid apologizing, justifying, or giving reasons. Focus on solutions.
- Express appreciation for all the feedback, not just the *negative part*. Leave the evaluator with the perception that you understood all of it, both negative and *positive*.

FOR EXAMPLE

Men may perceive that women cannot accept **negative feedback**. Ellie Raynolds, a partner at the headhunting firm Ward Howell International, said, "Corporate males still don't know how to deal with women. They are afraid...to give them negative feedback. It's as though they think they are yelling at their mothers." (*Fortune*, July 30, 1990)

CREDIBILITY

As we discussed in Chapter 1, your effectiveness as a communicator depends on the target audience's perception of your credibility. But our goal here is not just achieving credibility, which you will accomplish by applying the **CrossTalk** Communication Model. Rather, our concern is that men and women who exhibit the same behaviors and who are equal in terms of training, rank, and experience are often not *perceived* as equal.

Reviewing the Kenton Credibility Model in terms of this chapter summarizes the important points about gender differences in workplace communication.

Goodwill: The receivers' perception of the sender's focus on and concern for them.   Women have traditionally been afforded attention-*giving* roles, and men have traditionally been afforded attention-*getting* roles. As a result, both your male and female receivers expect that a woman will focus on them more than on herself.

However, if a man offers the same kind of nurturing and attention that is expected of a woman, he receives "extra points." The woman who does not meet expectations loses credibility. Although women may benefit from initial expectations that they will show goodwill, if they do not behave accordingly, receivers will judge them more harshly than they would men who behave exactly the same way.

FOR EXAMPLE

At the Southern Women in Public Service conference in Atlanta in May 1995, women from thirteen states met for nonpartisan networking. First Lady Hillary Rodham Clinton addressed the group, many of whom expressed appreciation for her powerful personal style. This discussion included comments about Clinton's style causing a negative reaction from her critics.

"She's a very successful woman in her own right," said Alabama State Treasurer Lucy Baxley in Clinton's defense. "If a man had realized her level of success, they wouldn't have expected *him* to be docile, quiet, and of no opinion on anything!"

If you are a woman, you should meet expectations that you will nurture your subordinates and show concern for your many audiences.

If you are a man, you should exceed expectations by expressing concern for your many audiences.

Expertise: The receivers' perception of the sender's education, knowledge, and experience.   Researchers have discovered that even when a man and woman possess equal expertise, both male and female receivers perceive the man as being the more qualified expert.

If you are a woman, take every opportunity to showcase your knowledge and experience, while being very careful not to appear boastful. See pages 19–20 in Chapter 1 for additional explanation.

FOR EXAMPLE

Sandra Kurtzig, founder of the ASK Group, and Charlotte Beers, CEO, Ogilvy and Mather Worldwide, learned early in their respective careers that knowledge and expertise were great equalizers.

Kurtiz summed it up this way: "After the guys, particularly the roll-up-your-shirt-sleeves manufacturing guys, realized I knew what I was talking about, I gained even more credibility than if I were a man. Once they recognized that I was good at what I did, they figured I was probably better than most men because of all the B.S. I had put up with." (*Computerworld*, March 21, 1994)

Beers reportedly (in slightly different versions from many sources) surprised a boardroom of men at J. Walter Thompson in 1974 by proving her expertise in a traditionally nonfeminine skill. While presenting a proposal for an advertising campaign, Beers adroitly dismantled and then reassembled a Sears drill. (We assume that the advertising campaign was *for* Sears drills.)

If you are a man, do not exaggerate your knowledge and experience at the risk of becoming unbelievable. Receivers will perceive your modesty as charming and persuasive.

Power: The receivers' perception of the sender's status and success.   Rank should correlate with perceptions of status, but researchers have found that when men and women have equal rank, audiences afford higher status to men. Success translates into others' perception of your power as well, but both men and women attribute a man's success to his ability and a woman's success to hard work and an easy task. In addition, audiences often perceive typically "masculine" behaviors, such as interrupting, controlling conversation, and occupying large amounts of space, as being more powerful.

However, women who employ "power behaviors" may confuse or alienate their target audiences. On the other hand, behaviors such as smiling and lingering eye contact often send mixed messages as well. One audience may perceive smiling women as expressing warmth. Another audience may assume that the same women are allowing domination when they smile, maintain eye contact (perceived as gazing adoringly), and allow their space to be invaded.

If you are a woman, expect to work harder in order to be perceived as equal to your male counterparts.

If you are a man, expect to perform to the high level of expectation of your audiences.

Self-presentation: The receivers' perception of the sender's communication skills and confidence.   The confidence with which you demonstrate your skills is the most important factor in the perception of your credibility by your audience. Men are socialized to be comfortable in front of groups, yet women's language skills are often more developed. Confidence in communication is a *major* expectation in the corporate arena.

Reality and personal experience teach us that being confident is not always easy. However, audiences tend to perceive women who do not appear confident as lacking ability. An uncomfortable man may be perceived as endearing, particularly by a female audience. (A male audience may not notice at all.)

If you are a woman, prepare and practice so that both your skills and your confidence as you demonstrate those skills are the best that they can be.

If you are a man, your confidence and extemporaneous abilities should not preclude careful preparation. You must select and organize information based on thorough audience analysis to maintain credibility.

In Summary

In the beginning, a man has credibility. He works to keep it. In the beginning, a woman has to work very hard to earn credibility. She works even harder to keep it.

Review Chapter 1 for information on improving skills that are necessary for all communicators. Review this chapter for gender-specific details.

In Conclusion

The problems that arise from differences in the perception of the credibility of men and women in the workplace are complex. So are the solutions. But the first step is to recognize that this is not a woman's issue; it is a corporate issue. Men, women, organizations, and business will benefit if men and women of equal rank, training, and expertise are afforded equal credibility.

On an individual level, we must recognize that men and women with roots in the European culture have been socialized to behave in particular ways and to expect certain behaviors from others. As male and female business communicators, we all have behavioral tendencies. As male and female audiences, we all have biases. If you believe differently, you need to raise your awareness.

For Example

We received this letter from Jennifer Dellapina, an M.B.A. candidate:

> I attended the Students for Responsible Business conference at Harvard Business School this past weekend. Each of the panelists had *many* stories, all recent, where they felt they were treated differently because of their gender. These anecdotes are all amazing; some are blatant and others are subtle, but it's still hard to believe these things are going on today.
>
> It may be true that employers will not pass us over simply because we are women (but it may *not* be true, either), but every day we are treated differently only because we are women. Every woman in the room had examples. It was enlightening…and emotional.

To be successful, a woman has to be better at her job than a man.

Golda Meir

Finally, as members of organizations, we have responsibilities. We must recognize both our strengths and weaknesses and those of others to create the greatest possible perception of personal and corporate credibility.

Suggested Readings on Gender Differences and the European Culture

Aries, E. "Gender and Communication." In P. Shaver and C. Hendrick (eds.) *Sex and Gender*, 149–176. Newbury Park, CA: Sage, 1987.

Carr-Ruffino, N. *Managing Cultural Differences*. Cincinnati, OH: Thomson Executive Press, 1996.

Carr-Ruffino, N. *The Promotable Woman*, 2nd ed. Belmont, CA: Wadsworth, 1993.

Harcourt, J., Krizan, A. C., and Merrier, P. *Business Communication*, 3rd ed. Cincinnati, OH: International Thomson Publishing, 1996.

Kenton, S. B. "Speaker Credibility in Persuasive Business Communication." *The Journal of Business Communication*, Vol. 26: 2, Spring 1989.

Scheele, A. *Career Strategies for the Working Woman*. New York: Simon & Schuster, 1994.

Tannen, D. *Talking 9 to 5*. New York: William Morrow, 1994.

Thiederman, S. *Profiting in America's Multicultural Marketplace*. New York: Macmillan, 1991.

CHAPTER 3

WHAT IF YOUR AUDIENCE HAS ROOTS IN THE AFRICAN CULTURE?

In the modern city, how we capitalize on our diversity is how well we'll come out.

HOUSTON MAYOR BOB LANIER (AFTER WINNING A 35 PERCENT INCREASE IN MINORITY CONTRACTING GOALS IN 1995)

Ethnic and cultural diversity can increase an organization's profitability and enrich our lives if we are open to the possibilities of reaching out and learning new ways of communicating. Consider the following:

- The African-American population of the United States today numbers some 30 million or 12.1 percent of the U.S. population (Census, 1993). African Americans represent our largest ethnic group.

- The African continent represents a vast market. Yet a United Nations study (*Foreign Direct Investment in Africa*, 1995) reports new foreign direct investments to Africa's developing countries have slipped to 5 percent annually, from roughly 11 percent in the 1980s. Ironically, the report also shows that Africa's return on investment by American companies totaled an impressive 25 percent in 1993.

Thus, understanding the communication styles of audiences with roots in the African culture will help businesses:

- Manage African-American employees
- Understand African-American managers
- Explore untapped markets both domestically and on the African continent
- Promote acceptance of ethnic diversity

 We will highlight differences between cities or countries within the greater culture within boxes marked with an icon that denotes "Intracultural Notes."

Whether dealing with African-American customers, clients, or colleagues or learning ways to invest in the many developing markets of the African continent, we must **CrossTalk** our messages in order to be effective. We can overcome cultural differences with an audience rooted in the African culture by following the **CrossTalk** Communication Model outlined in Chapter 1 (see pages 1–20).

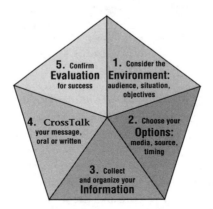

CONSIDER THE ENVIRONMENT

 With people rooted in the African culture, as with every audience, we begin with step one of the **CrossTalk** Communication Model: **consider the environment**. We will first examine specific characteristics of **audiences** with roots in the African culture and then discuss your **situation** and **objectives**.

ANALYZE YOUR AUDIENCE

When you speak to other businesspeople about your plans to communicate with an African or African-American audience or conduct library research, keep a copy of the **Audience Analysis Worksheet** with you (Appendix B). Fill in general information about your audience as you interview or read.

As always, the following characteristics provide only broad markers for understanding people from an African culture. These markers should not lead you to a generalized view of your audience. When working through the chapter, remember that individuals within this culture will display a range of variables in terms of attitudes and behavior. The information you collect for the Audience Analysis Worksheet will help you understand which of the following descriptions may apply to your specific audience.

Identify all potential audiences: primary, hidden, and decision makers. Initially, you will focus on your **primary audience**, the individual or group with roots in the African culture to whom you actually address your message. Perhaps you wish to open a retail outlet in Soweto, South Africa, an area of economic empowerment since the end of apartheid. Or maybe the ethnic diversity of your employee credit union based in Los Angeles is now 45 percent African American, and you want to improve the relationship and communication process between this population and that of the other diverse cultures. What do you need to know?

FOR EXAMPLE

Sanlam Properties, one of South Africa's largest commercial developers, built the $12.1 million Dobsonville Shopping Center in the heart of Soweto, South Africa (population 4 million). According to *Business Week* (September 25, 1995), after one year in business, the center's white managers admitted that their lack of understanding of black consumers' demands had caused glitches.

Sanlam could have been successful earlier if they had taken the time to identify and understand their **primary audience**. Sanlam's regional property manager, Swani Swanipole, says, "Everyone is watching with four eyes" to see if the venture can produce a profit.

Your **hidden audience** may be your manager or others who may hear or read your message. This secondary or hidden audience can present additional challenges because their characteristics may differ from those of your primary audience. If your hidden audience has roots in other cultures, refer to the appropriate chapter. If the diversity seems overwhelming, focus on characteristics your diverse audience may have in common.

The **decision maker** presents yet another challenge in audience analysis. Because this individual or group (whether internal or external) may hear your message through other sources, you will need to think about the characteristics of this audience as well. Also consider that your primary audience may be responsible for delivering your message to the decision maker. Therefore, the primary audience will both need to understand your message and be able to effectively communicate it to the decision maker.

Investigate and learn about each audience. We will first examine **facts** to help you better analyze your audience with roots in the African culture. Consider the following possible African core **beliefs** and cultural **values** that influence communication **attitudes** and **behaviors**:

1. Holistic world view
2. Emotional and expressive
3. Keen sense of justice or fairness
4. Belief in the uniqueness of the individual as defined by the ethnic group

Notice how each core belief affects the following **attitudes** and the resulting communication **behaviors**:

1. Holistic world view
   - Sees the "big picture" rather than events in isolation

FOR EXAMPLE

For many, the O. J. Simpson trial symbolized racial strife. One University of North Carolina professor of communication studies has an alternative view as articulated in his book, *Between God and Gangsta Rap: Bearing Witness to Black Culture.*

Expressing a more **holistic viewpoint**, Michael Eric Dyson sees hope in the Simpson trial:

> Its major players are a virtual rainbow of color, gender, ethnicity, and class. Judge Lance Ito is Asian American. Johnnie Cochran is African American. Marcia Clark is a white woman. And Robert Shapiro, like Clark, is Jewish. A judicial landmark [was] constructed by people who a few decades ago couldn't stand equally together in the same court.

(Books, "Open Heart, Open Arms," *Time*, December 18, 1995)

 Twice-widowed Myrlie Evers-Williams, Chairperson of the NAACP National Board of Directors, exemplifies the **holistic world view** and emphasis on past and present family relationships. Evers-Williams claims that her work is made easier by two special powers, her deceased husbands. The October 1995 issue of *Ebony* quoted her as saying, "I don't get an answer [to difficult dilemmas]. I just get a gentle push from Medgar on one side and Walter on the other."

Present, past, and future blend into one for some African Americans, and even the beliefs of relatives who have passed on may influence decision making and communication behaviors.

   - Deals with times, numbers, and measurements in a relaxed way
   - May use flexible approximations rather than absolutes

2. Emotional and expressive
   - Is acutely aware of feelings and emotions
   - Values close relationships and family

FOR EXAMPLE

In the September 25, 1995, issue of *Business Week*, the Executive Director of the Soweto Chamber of Commerce, Max Legodi, recommends hiring black managers and staff and making a visible contribution to the neighborhood: "You must develop a partnership with the community."

Legodi believes the emphasis on a partnership or **relationships** between the various cultural elements of the community will contribute to business success.

   - Uses body language, non-verbal communication extensively

3. Keen sense of justice and fairness
   - Focuses on relationships rather than tasks or possessions

---

FOR EXAMPLE

African American Ann Fudge, President of Maxwell House Coffee and ranked as one of the fifteen most powerful women in America, **focuses on relationships** in her job. She is widely known for taking the time to help others unleash their potential.

Employees speak of the "liberating confidence" she has in their work and the example she sets in balancing her life as both an executive and a mother. (*Glamour,* December, 1995)

   - Expresses outrage at perceived personal offenses
   - Desires to be authentic, direct, and assertive

4. Belief in uniqueness of the individual as defined by the ethnic group
   - Prefers novelty and freedom in communication, dress, and music
   - Desires self-revelation within the ethnic group
   - Wants others to reveal themselves in communication exchanges

---

Bessie and Sadie Delany became best-selling authors after age 100 with their memoirs of growing up African American. They titled their book *Having Our Say,* after Miss Bessie's favorite phrase.

One a dentist and the other a science teacher, they lived together all of their lives. When asked how they had lived so long, Miss Sadie expressed both **assertiveness** and **self-revelation** when she answered, "Honey, we never married; we never had husbands to worry us to death." (*Atlanta Journal,* September 26, 1995)

We offer the preceding information as mere starting points for intercultural awareness when communicating with individuals with roots in the African culture.

Because individuals within the culture may vary widely, the next step of information gathering is necessary. You will find that sharing information (desire for self-revelation) is important for most individuals with roots in the African culture. Therefore, you will be able to discover specific **facts** about these individuals within the African culture through both the grapevine and preliminary conversations. Using the Audience Analysis Sheet (Appendix B), record the following specific information about your audience:

1. Gender
2. Education

Twelve percent of African-American women hold bachelor's or higher degrees as of the 1993 census. In addition, there are university-educated women in almost every African nation.

3. Job responsibilities and status
4. Civic and religious affiliations
5. Age or generation
6. Family or other personal information
7. Prior knowledge of your topic or business

The core **beliefs** of those rooted in the African culture and specific **facts** about your individual audiences will help you analyze possible **attitudes** about **you**, about your **topic**, and about **being there** to hear your message.

In considering their **attitude about you** as a EuroAmerican, for example, your audience may be concerned that you will:

- Reject their opinions
- Take advantage of them or hold them back
- Exclude them from full participation in decision making
- Consider them different in a negative way
- Put them in a weak negotiating position
- Fail to encourage them to achieve
- Deny them equal opportunities
- Portray them negatively in the white-dominated media

Barbara Arwine, Executive Director of the Lawyers Committee for Civil Rights Under Law, says, "Black women have been portrayed as welfare queens, drug abusers, and lazy. But African-American women have the same workforce participation rates as white women. We work longer hours, we work more days, we work harder jobs, and we make less pay." (*Atlanta Journal*, June 17, 1995)

What are their **attitudes about your message** and **about being there** to receive it? For example, consider the following questions:

1. Are they reluctant to meet with you, or are they eager to develop a relationship?
2. Do they have preconceived beliefs about your motives for wanting to meet?
3. Will they think you may not take them seriously or show them proper respect?

Determine their wants over your needs.   Those with roots in the African culture will want to establish a trusting relationship with you before true communication can begin. If you do not feel comfortable or qualified to build trust because of cultural differences, you should find a credible representative to do so.

Finally, as you get to know your African or African-American audience, you will begin to recognize their consistent and recurring **concerns**. These concerns are individual and will be based on how well you know them and their core beliefs. As with other audiences, the individuals in your African audience may have fundamental fears that they express in many situations. Look for recurring themes such as the fear of being in a weak negotiating position or uncertainty about your possible feelings of prejudice.

Refer to the **CrossTalk** Quick Chart in Appendix A for brief information on cultural differences.

ANALYZE YOUR SITUATION

Identify and define the problem.   Perhaps your company has recently hired several Nairobi accountants, and you want to help them successfully acclimate to your corporate culture. You may have heard that Kenya offers excellent opportunities for cellular phone sales. Or perhaps your company has been successful in increasing the number of African-American managers, and you wonder how to promote effective and open channels of communication among the resulting diverse group. Carefully defining your communication problem will help you progress through the communication model.

Evaluate the corporate culture of the African firm.   People from the African culture are very concerned with the well-being of the family and their ethnic group, which is similar to an extended family. Such an attitude carries over into businesses where workers develop loyalty to an ethnic leader or the equivalent (many times a spiritual or political leader). Because of this loyalty, an African or African American may trust the advice of family, friends, or spiritual or political leaders, regardless of information available to them through the mass media.

FOR EXAMPLE

When African American General Colin Powell announced he would not run for president of the United States, he made his decision despite polls that showed he would probably win.
"I have spent long hours talking with my wife and children, the most important people in my life....The welfare of my **family** had to be uppermost in my mind...." (*Atlanta Journal*, November 9, 1995)

Even in the United States, the corporate culture of an African-American firm may be based on loyalty to leaders and a trusting relationship with both leaders and co-workers.

In the United States, African-American women are more visible in the managerial ranks than ever before, thanks in part to affirmative action initiatives and higher levels of education.
In addition, more and more African-American women are tapping into networks such as the Corporate Women's Network (CWN), which has been bringing black corporate women together since 1974.

Assess the external climate.   Read industry-specific journals as well as national newspapers to learn about the external climate of your industry in the United States. Take advantage of the many conferences and conventions in your industry to learn about trends and forecasts.

If you plan to do business with firms located on the African continent, your task will be harder, but not impossible. Many resources are available to help you learn about the external climate of a specific industry abroad. Consult the resources listed below.

1. **NewsNet** (800-952-0122) provides information on the following online publications: *Africa News On-Line, Investest/African Region, Monthly Regional Bulletin, PRS Forecasts: Mid-East and North Africa, PRS Forecasts: Sub-Saharan Africa, Southern Africa Business Intelligence.*

2. **The United Nations Library** (212-963-7394 or -7395) provides copies of economic reports on various African states.

Two African Americans have taken advantage of a favorable **external climate** in the United States in two diverse industries: home health-care and telecommunications.

- Even though the home-care industry has grown to 17,561 agencies today from 11,097 in 1989, according to the National Association for Home Care in Washington, D.C., ethnic communities continue to be underserved. Seeing a need for minority home health-care, African American Carolyn Colby founded Colby Care Nurses Inc. in 1988. The company provides home health-care services to clients in Los Angeles County, most of whom are black or Latino.

- Small communities have more telecommunications resources than corporations to utilize them. Omaha-based NCS International Inc., led by CEO James Beatty, strives to match corporate telecommunications needs with community resources—especially small communities heavily populated by minorities. Beatty, who is African-American, seeks to bridge the gap between corporate America and minority communities. The external climate has remained favorable since the company's inception in 1989, with corporate profits up 20 percent in 1995. (*The Wall Street Journal*, October 19, 1995)

3. **The African Studies Center** of local colleges or universities provides magazines that focus on Africa (*West Africa, BBC's Focus on Africa, Jeune Afrique*), as well as academic papers relating to issues affecting Africans and African Americans.

4. **The Internet** will connect you to networks offered by twenty African countries. The African Studies Center can provide Internet addresses.

5. **The Chamber of Commerce** in your area supplies information about organizations designed to help American businesses succeed abroad.

6. **Your local university** can provide names of professors or foreign exchange students in the M.B.A. program who can provide information on a particular country. (The university is also a good source for interpreters.)

7. **The embassy** of the African country in Washington, D.C., will supply helpful information.

Consult the Embassy of South Africa at 3051 Massachusetts Ave., NW, Washington, D.C., 29998, or call 202-232-4400.

8. **The U.S. Department of Commerce International Trade Administration** (800-USA-TRADE) will give information on marketing the types of goods or services you represent.

9. **The Export-Import Bank of the United States (Eximbank)** (202-565-3946) provides information on financing exports.

FOR EXAMPLE

When researching the **external corporate climate** of an African business, you will learn that telephone services are still developing in Africa. Line density averages 2.3 per 100 people compared with 50 per 100 people in the United States (Robert S. Fortner, *International Communication*, 1993). In addition, the lack of adequate roads creates transportation problems, including inconsistent mail delivery. Take these issues into account as you plan your communication.

External culture influences your communication decisions. Use the numbered resources to fully research this aspect of culture. In addition, consult the suggested readings on the African culture at the end of this chapter.

When researching the **external culture**, you will find interesting contradictions. For example, in some African countries such as Malawi, lineage is traced through the mother's side of the family rather than the father's (matrilineal rather than patrilineal), which gives women added economic and social power.

However, in other African countries such as Kenya, women work an average of fifty-six hours per week to earn what a man does in only forty-two hours. Even though African women have a long way to go to achieve parity with men, experts predict that the situation for women will improve over the next few decades as investment and development in Africa grow.

ANALYZE YOUR OBJECTIVES

You will next look at your objectives and how they relate to your audience with roots in the African culture. Remember from Chapter 1 that your objectives include **an overall goal, a specific purpose of the communication**, and **a hidden agenda**.

Your **overall goal** is influenced by the mission statement of your company. For example, your mission statement may include the goal of establishing international networks or diversifying your customer base. In addition, look for phrases in your mission statement that would particularly appeal to your African or African-American colleague or client, and include those phrases in your message.

FOR EXAMPLE

The following excerpt from a **mission statement** will be a useful tool in recruiting employees with roots in the African culture because it emphasizes the uniqueness of each individual within the group: "We believe in the individuality of each worker within our organization as well as the individual needs of each customer."

The **specific purpose of your communication** is the actual reason you are writing or speaking. Recognize that although African markets are open and growing, it will take time to make the necessary connections to begin moving products across borders. Therefore, your specific purpose might be to immediately open lines of communication with the target markets, perhaps by joining a trade mission organized by your city or state government. We recommend that you increase by one-third the time you usually allocate for achieving joint ventures, depending on the particular African country's negotiating style.

FOR EXAMPLE

African American Michelle Greenidge Joiner of Decatur, Georgia, traveled to South Africa on a city-sponsored trade mission in April 1995. Before the trip, she carefully defined her **specific purpose**: to find a South African company willing to open primary health care clinics there as a joint venture.

By September, even though several potential problems still needed to be considered, Joiner reported, "At this point, it appears that [negotiations] will come to a fruitful end."

Finally, what is your **hidden agenda**? Everyone has a hidden agenda, and recognizing yours can help prevent problems. Perhaps you've always wanted to travel to Africa to expand your customer base. If you advocate a fast move into the African market because of your hidden agenda, you and your company may be disappointed. Other hidden agendas may include the desire for personal growth, for increasing diversity in the company, or for simply increasing the profit of your department.

CHOOSE YOUR OPTIONS

After analyzing your audience, situation, and objectives, you are ready to consider your communication options. Remember that your *receiver's* wants and needs will influence your choices of **medium, source,** and **timing**.

MEDIA OPTIONS: HOW SHOULD THE MESSAGE BE SENT?

The African culture believes in the power and force of verbal communication. Historically, people selected leaders on the basis of their abilities to communicate creatively, rhythmically, and forcefully with the spoken word (*Nommo*). Both African and African-American listeners seek to become one with the speaker by responding actively. This coincides with the African core belief in the interrelatedness of all things—the holistic world view mentioned earlier.

FOR EXAMPLE

Lynell George of the *Los Angeles Times* wrote a definitive article about African-American communication patterns (November 25, 1993). After describing the scene at 5th Street Dick's, a meeting spot where neighbors gather to share information, George wrote:

> Many blacks have long sought that second source to confirm the headlines or flesh out what passed like a dream in a brief sound bite over the airwaves....
>
> For many blacks, oral testimonies are the sole repository of the precious details, the place where the history is locked tight and hidden from harm....the ritual of sharing stories, allegories, warnings, histories, and sometimes rumors at an appointed time and place has historically been a way of rallying support, asserting pride, and passing the culture....

In the United States, we are familiar with the call and response patterns of the African-American churches. Black political leaders also use the interactive pattern of communication to lead and convince the audience.

When choosing media options, therefore, the spoken word will take precedence over the written word. Place extra emphasis on selecting your **speaking options** with the African audience, since the spoken word carries significant weight.

Speaking options.   Consider the following when selecting your speaking options.

* **Grapevine**. Heavily used by both African and African-American cultures. Word of mouth is an excellent way to find out informal information about your potential customer, client, or colleague or to disseminate information.

FOR EXAMPLE

Successful entrepreneur Phil Hagans, an African American who owns two McDonald's franchises in Houston, understands the preference many blacks have for information gathered through the **grapevine**. Therefore, instead of advertising in the newspaper or television, he wisely chose a more trusted method of increasing business.

Hagans personally visited churches and day-care centers and encouraged people to hold birthday parties and meetings in his restaurant. As word of mouth carried his message, sales doubled. (*The Wall Street Journal*, August 23, 1995)

- **Conversation**. Extremely important in communicating with an audience rooted in the African culture. Strive to be open, direct, and genuine in your informal conversations, and expect the same from your African or African-American counterpart.
- **Interview**. Best conducted via an interpreter unless your African counterpart speaks English fluently. Prepare to answer as many questions as you ask. Convey an attitude of genuine concern.
- **Phone call or teleconference**. Can be helpful if well planned. Allow extra time for phone conversations with African Americans to establish your authenticity, understanding, and acceptance. Call your long-distance company for information on obtaining interpreters who speak the language of business in the African country you have selected. Less developed areas have few phone lines, so prepare an alternative method of communication as well.
- **Meeting**. The primary way to establish a trusting relationship and subsequently conduct business. Open debate and argument are ways of achieving consensus and should not be taken personally.
- **Formal presentation**. Should be interactive. Allow time throughout for questions and responses. Be prepared to respond to objections or concerns that are voiced openly, and do not take objections or arguments personally.

FOR EXAMPLE

African American Jack Davenport discusses the interaction between speaker and listener: "I just like people and I enjoy **arguing**....Sometimes I know they're right, but I won't say it that way. To me, that is the only way that you learn...by discussing things." (*Los Angeles Times*, November 25, 1993)

Select more than one speaking option when communicating with African or African-American businesspeople. The oral tradition in the African culture is powerful and respected. You will establish trust with your African or African-American audience by speaking powerfully and confidently.

Writing options.   Consider the following when selecting your writing options:
- **Greeting card**. After establishing a relationship with individuals with roots in the African culture, it is appropriate to send greeting cards (see National Holidays in Appendix L).
- **Business card**. Imprint on both sides: one in English and the other in the language of the specific African country you visit.

Be aware that Africa is the "continent of 1,000 languages." In Zaire alone, at least 200 languages are spoken. Where there is competition and rivalry between ethnic groups, it would be a serious mistake to print your **business card** in the wrong language.

- **Letter, memo, fax, or electronic mail.** Strive to achieve warmth in your correspondence, but maintain a degree of formality. Never use first names. Double-check spelling of names, and make sure you use the acceptable form of address for the specific country. Note that phonetic translations of some African names will take more than one acceptable form (see Appendix I).

- **Report.** Use a written report to support both informal conversations and formal presentations. Your detailed information and statistics belong there.

SOURCE OPTIONS: WHO SHOULD DELIVER THE MESSAGE?

Your best choice to deliver your message will be a man or woman who uses language with creativity and conviction. In addition, select an individual who is respected and trusted by the community.

For a foreign audience, select an interpreter you know and trust. Call the African Studies Center at a local university to obtain a list of possible interpreters. Spend time with the individual you select to establish common goals and understanding.

An African Studies Center is also an excellent source of information on consultants specializing in the African country you have selected. A consultant can help you select your source option (the person who will deliver your message).

FOR EXAMPLE

Brooklyn Bottling faced a crisis in March 1991. An unknown enemy of the company spread rumors that its highly successful soft drink, Tropical Fantasy, was actually manufactured by the Ku Klux Klan and would result in the sterilization of African-American men who drank it.

The company wisely chose a leading member of the African-American community as the **source** of their message. New York Mayor David Dinkins agreed to appear on television and drink the product to demonstrate its safety (*The Wall Street Journal*, May 10, 1991).

TIMING OPTIONS: WHEN SHOULD THE MESSAGE ARRIVE?

Other cultures view time itself differently. Cultures can be described as polychronic or monochronic. (Polychronic societies see time as flexible and fluid. Monochronic societies such as the United States tend to see time as a tangible entity to be spent, saved, or lost. For more information, see the Comparative Time Orientation Chart in Appendix A.)

Individuals with roots in the African culture view time more in the past and present than in the distant future. (In fact, many African languages do not have a future tense.) Being polychronic, the African culture sees time as fluid and flexible rather than as an entity to be saved, spent, or budgeted.

With all polychronic cultures, be flexible when negotiating deadlines for shipments or completion of construction projects. Indeed, allow more time for the entire process of doing business.

COLLECT AND ORGANIZE YOUR INFORMATION

 As with most other matters, individuals with roots in the African culture may prefer a particular style of organization (see Appendix D for several flexible options). Here are some guidelines that apply to most messages:

- **Consider culture-specific and gender-specific information** by paying close attention to the advice in this chapter.

- **Plan a beginning, a middle, and an end**, but be sure to give the African audience an overview or roadmap of your message. They will be interested in the big picture.

- **Emphasize the expertise** you and your company can offer, and cite appropriate examples.

- **Limit main points.** Instead of trying to cover many points briefly, discuss one or two issues in more depth.

- **Limit your agenda to one issue**, but allow time to discuss matters of importance that will strengthen your relationship with the African audience.

- **Enhance your message with visual aids, numbers, and examples.** Colorful report covers, charts, and graphs will add vitality to your presentation or written report. Through your research of the external climate and history of the specific country, identify the best color combinations. Convert to metric where applicable.

- **Use imagery, simile, and metaphor** for greater impact with your African audience. Illustrate your main points with colorful stories and anecdotes.

FOR EXAMPLE

Consider these images from the Reverend Jesse Jackson's speech at the Million Man March in Washington, D.C., on October 16, 1995:

> How good it is to hear the sounds of chains and shackles breaking from the ankles and minds of men. How beautiful it is to see the rejected stones stand up, become the cornerstones of a new spiritual and social order.
> But I tell you today, rabbit hunting ain't fun when the rabbits stop running and start fighting back.

- **Tailor your message to your individual audience.** Research your target audience, and include specific references to the African company. Remember that the information we offer you is designed as a guide, not a rulebook. Within every business and every culture, each person is unique.

CrossTalk YOUR MESSAGE, ORAL OR WRITTEN

When we say **CrossTalk** your message, we are referring to the accommodations you will need to make to better communicate with an audience from a different culture.

ORAL MESSAGES

If you are preparing to speak to your African or African-American audience (an individual or a group), follow these guidelines:

1. **Dress appropriately** as a sign of respect (business suit and tie; skirted suit for women).

2. **Warm up your body, face, and voice** to enhance physical and vocal variety.

3. **Use appropriate eye contact** by looking at each person individually as you talk. Remember that African Americans tend to gaze steadily while speaking and look away while listening, a pattern that is reversed by EuroAmericans. Finally, direct your comments to the audience rather than the interpreter, if you use one.

African-American women look at their conversational partners less and lean toward each other more than EuroAmerican women.

4. **Vary your rate and volume of delivery** for appropriate emphasis. Use greater volume to stress important points.

5. **Reduce physical barriers**, such as stationary microphones. Your African audience may welcome a greater closeness than we usually establish in the United States. Such closeness varies somewhat from country to country throughout Africa.

6. **Move naturally.** Effective gestures can be large and sweeping, but only if you are practiced and comfortable using them (see **CrossTalk** Your Messages, Oral or Written, in Chapter 1).

7. **Show your audience that you care.** Your audience will be looking for a personal commitment from you. Be excited about your message, and your African or African-American audience will respond accordingly.

WRITTEN MESSAGES

The following list includes some general advice for writing or transmitting electronically to an African audience. (Be aware, though, that electronic transmissions may be monitored by the government of the African nation.)

1. **Use the Outline Worksheet (Appendix C).** In addition, after analyzing your African or African-American reader, write the most difficult sentences first. These could include initial, final, or bad news sentences.

2. **Write as naturally as you speak** for your African-American audience. In addition, use the most common definition of a word to assist the African businessperson who might be consulting a dictionary to translate English.

3. **Avoid two-word verbs** when writing in English to an African audience. Rather than writing, "Please *back up* your statement with more details," you might try, "Please *support* your statement with more details."

4. **Use a single page** whenever possible for most business communication such as letters, memos, and electronic mail for both your African and African-American receivers. Use an executive summary to cover longer reports. If your English will be translated into an African language, keep in mind that the resulting letter or other written communication will be longer.

5. **Avoid idiomatic expressions.** When writing for the African audience or your interpreter, strive to write clearly by avoiding slang, jargon, and acronyms. If your reader would not be familiar with your industry-related acronyms, write them out the first time, and then type the acronym in parentheses.

6. **In a longer paper, use headings and subheadings**, in addition to bullet points, graphs, and charts, to guide your African or African-American reader through your information.

7. **Read aloud** as part of your preparation for the African-American reader. Does your report or letter sound sincere? Do you convey your commitments forcefully? For your African reader, try to imagine yourself as a speaker of another language. Is there anything that might be confusing? Instruct your translator to follow this step as well.

8. **Cross-translate** crucial documents such as contracts. Begin with written English. After the document is translated into the native African language, ask someone who is bilingual (not the original translator) to translate it back into English. Compare the cross-translation to the original English version for accuracy of key points.

CONFIRM EVALUATION FOR SUCCESS

Unlike other cultures, where individuals may appear to agree with you to preserve harmony, the audience with roots in the African culture will let you know whether they agree or disagree with various points. Your success will depend on how well you listen, ask questions, and accept responsibility.

When evaluating feedback from an African or African-American audience:

1. **Listen carefully to comments.** Be aware of a difference in listening behavior. The African or African-American listener may look away rather than at you while listening.

If you find your business deal is not accepted, ask for referrals to other firms who may be interested. Africans and African Americans typically understand and use networking.

FOR EXAMPLE

Although **networking** may be conducted on an informal basis, increasingly in the United States, there are organized groups to assist. These include the National Association of Black Women Entrepreneurs, the Association of African and American Black Business People, the National Black MBA Association, and the National Minority Supplier Development Council.

---

2. **Paraphrase to confirm meaning.** Also try the phrase, "Tell me more." The African or African-American audience will appreciate the fact that you keep trying to understand as a mark of your sincerity.

3. **Correct in the *direction* of the evaluation** given by your African or African-American audience. If you have roots in the European culture, you will never be African or African American. However, you can best strive to convey your acceptance and understanding of the needs of the African culture by genuinely being yourself.

4. **Look for it in writing.** In the African culture, giving your "word" is as important as writing your signature. For the African-American culture, your legal signature represents your commitment to perform honorably.

5. **Recognize that your audience's perceptions define reality.** For example, your African or African-American audience may feel you have spoken from the head and not the heart. If so, you must strive to correct this opinion in future communication.

6. **Remember to thank your evaluator.** Negative feedback is as difficult to give as to receive. If you receive no feedback from your African or African-American audience, you can be sure you failed to communicate effectively. Be sure to thank them, and try again.

In the report of an extensive study of African-American career women, E. L. Bell summarized black women's responses to white co-workers. The **feedback** from your female African-American audience might be influenced by these same attitudes and behaviors:

"I never talk much or laugh. I am stiff, reserved, and cautious. When I am with whites, I hold back on my emotions, and I watch my body language. I am usually pretty conscious of my behavior." (*Journal of Organizational Behavior*, Vol. 11, p. 474)

CREDIBILITY

Building credibility with your African or African-American colleagues, clients, or customers will take time, commitment, and sincerity. Your knowledge of their expectations is the most effective and efficient tool you can employ. (Refer to the Kenton Credibility Model on page 19 in Chapter 1.)

You will achieve the perception of **goodwill** by taking enough time to build a relationship based on trust. As your business relationship progresses, your audience will perceive your goodwill as you express it in both word and deed.

You will achieve the perception of **expertise** by presenting evidence of prior success in similar ventures. The African or African-American audience will expect you to detail your prior success and the success of your company in performing well.

You will achieve the perception of **power** through choosing a credible spokesperson. Remember that this culture reveres age and respects a person's ability to talk eloquently and passionately.

You will achieve the perception of effective **self-presentation** by laying the groundwork, knowing the culture, and presenting with eloquence, energy, and style. With the African or African-American audience, remember to **CrossTalk** your message for optimum results.

IN CONCLUSION

In summary, on October 16, 1995, the day of the Million Man March in Washington, D.C., President Clinton spoke in Austin, Texas. The Associated Press reported this excerpt:

> White Americans and black Americans often see the world in drastically different ways....The reasons for this divide are many....Some are rooted in the different ways we experience the threats of modern life to personal security, family values, and strong communities. Some are rooted in the fact that we still haven't learned to talk frankly, to listen carefully....

CrossTalk is our effort to help all of us better understand the cultural issues that have divided us. Through understanding, we will begin to communicate more effectively.

The namer of names is the parent of things.

AFRICAN PROVERB

Suggested Readings on the African Culture

Bell, Ella Louise. "The Bicultural Life Experience of Career-Oriented Black Women." *Journal of Organizational Behavior*, Vol. 11, 459–477. 1990.

Carr-Ruffino, N. *Managing Cultural Differences*. Cincinnati, OH: Thomson Executive Press, 1996.

deVillers, Les, and others. *Doing Business with South Africa*. New Canaan, CT: Business Books International, 1986.

Dyson, Michael Eric. *Between God and Gangsta Rap: Bearing Witness to Black Culture*. New York: Oxford Press, 1995.

Hecht, Michael L., and others. *African American Communication*. Newberry Park, CA: Sage, 1993.

Turner, Patricia A. *I Heard it Through the Grapevine*. Los Angeles: University of California Press, 1995.

CHAPTER

4

WHAT IF YOUR AUDIENCE HAS ROOTS IN THE ASIAN CULTURE?

What we need in business is to be able to think like a Japanese and speak English, rather than think like an American and speak Japanese.

ROBERTO GOIZUETA, CEO, COCA-COLA

Businesspeople in the United States believe if they could only "speak the language" of an Asian country, all of their communication problems would be solved. However, even one who is fluent in Japanese or Hindi can make grievous errors by failing to understand how culture affects communication styles. In this chapter, we will answer the question, "What if your audience (the individual or group who receives your oral or written communication) is Asian or has roots in the Asian culture?"

We will highlight differences between cities or countries within the greater culture within boxes marked with an icon (◐) that denotes "Intracultural Notes."

Although more than thirty countries can be considered Asian, for this discussion we are including China (People's Republic of China, mainland China, Hong Kong), Malaysia, Southeast Asia (Laos, Thailand, Cambodia, Vietnam), Japan, India, and Korea (North and South Korea). In addition, we are including Asian Americans (numbering seven million or 3 percent of the U.S. population in 1990) who continue to be influenced by their native culture.

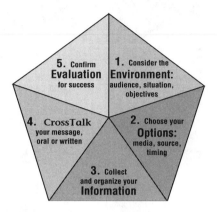

CONSIDER THE ENVIRONMENT

With individuals from the Asian culture, as with every audience, we begin with step one of the **CrossTalk** Communication Model: Consider the environment, which consists of analyzing your audience, situation, and objectives.

ANALYZE YOUR AUDIENCE

When you speak to other businesspeople about your plans or do library research, use a copy of the Audience Analysis Worksheet (Appendix B). Fill in general information about your Asian audience as you read. Be careful, however, because no two individuals in any culture will be exactly the same.

Consider that being direct and to the point is considered rude in the Asian business world where relationships rule. Therefore, U.S. businesspeople need to slow down and take time to establish trust with potential Asian customers, clients, or suppliers. Remember to begin every communication with pleasant information about the weather or sports, or inquire about the general well-being of your Asian or Asian-American audience.

FOR EXAMPLE

You will be surprised if you fail to expect **individual differences** in the Asian or Asian-American audience. Even though most Japanese prefer an indirect style of communication, some individuals choose a direct style *because* it is unexpected.

In the recent trade dispute between Japan and the United States, Japan's Liberal Democratic Party (LDP), leaders became unhappy with Trade & Industry Minister Ryutaro Hashimoto because of his use of a more direct or Western style of negotiating.

During the automobile trade talks with the United States, Hashimoto treated the U.S. trade negotiator somewhat irreverently. Although winning points with the Japanese public, Hashimoto's direct speaking damaged his credibility within the party. (*Business Week,* July 24, 1995)

Completing the Audience Analysis Worksheet will provide a good start toward understanding your individual audience. Revise it as you participate in meetings and socialize with your Asian audience.

Identify all potential audiences: primary, hidden, and decision makers. Identifying your primary, hidden, and decision-making audiences when you are communicating with an Asian firm is an extremely critical step. Many times, because of your position in your own company, you will not be able to write or speak directly with the decision maker. You may be of lower rank and would therefore be expected to contact someone on the same horizontal level as you. That person (your primary audience) will present your proposal.

The time you devote to developing the relationship with your primary audience (your personal counterpart in an Asian firm and the one who will receive your message) will determine the way your message is conveyed to the decision maker. Failure to devote an adequate amount of time to nurturing the business relationship will be interpreted as rude and will negatively affect the outcome of your goals.

Your hidden audience is the team or group to which the Asian representative belongs. If your early contacts are by telephone, you might easily overlook this hidden audience. Be aware of the presence of a team that will immediately receive information and impressions about you.

Investigate and learn about each audience.   After you have identified your Asian audiences, try to learn personal and professional **facts** about them that will help you understand their **attitudes, wants,** and **concerns.** Do not be too direct in asking for information. Ask a secondary source whenever possible, and always phrase questions politely.

Fill in the Audience Analysis Sheet, including both professional and personal **facts** such as age, gender, education, job responsibilities and status, civic and religious affiliations, and their prior knowledge of your topic.

Most Asians may not be comfortable discussing personal matters until they trust you. Even then, they may share this type of information only at social gatherings. Such outings provide an opportunity to ask polite questions and engage in conversation that will help you know important facts about your audience.

As you conduct your factual analysis, consider the following possible Asian core beliefs and cultural values that influence communication attitudes and behaviors:

1. Group orientation
2. Respect for hierarchy
3. Sensitivity to feelings of self and others (saving face)
4. Desire for harmony
5. Belief in fatalism

Each core belief affects the following **attitudes** and the resulting communication **behaviors**:

1. Group orientation
   - Favors the needs of the group over the individual
   - Believes in loyalty, cooperation, and obedience
   - Works hard to achieve group goals
   - Prefers "we, us, ours" to "I, me, mine"
   - Values group reward; avoids individual reward

The traditional structure of the Asian family exemplifies core beliefs of group orientation and respect for authority.

In a 1992 poll of 1,000 Japanese women by the Tokyo City government, 56 percent agreed that "the husband should be the breadwinner and the wife should stay at home."

In similar polls, just 13 percent of Swedish women thought wives should stay at home as did 20 percent of British women, 22 percent of French women, 24 percent of American women, and 25 percent of German women. (*The Wall Street Journal*, July 26, 1995)

2. Respect for hierarchy
   - Believes each person has a place in a vertical hierarchy
   - Requires formality in relationships
   - Adheres to rules of behavior (obedience)
   - Strives toward high education as an investment in family status
   - Shows respect for age, tenure, authority

3. Sensitivity to feelings of self and others (saving face)
   - Is concerned with preserving dignity and face
   - Experiences loss of face if the "boss" helps do the work
   - Takes job performance review personally
   - Values fairness more than wealth
   - Expresses opinions indirectly

For Example

Carnegie Mellon Professor of Management Communication, Evelyn Pierce, Ph.D., has observed the following communication behaviors:

> While our Asian executive education students seem bound by their need to save face and preserve honor, their desire for honesty is slightly different. After the necessary relationship building, when they are ready to discuss an issue more directly, we should not continue to be indirect.
>
> They may become very annoyed if native English speakers seem to contradict themselves. So I've found that with complicated issues, I have to make subtle differences very clear and definite.

4. Desire for harmony
   - Does not easily interrupt others
   - Prefers not to be interrupted while speaking
   - Avoids conflict in communication
   - Shows self-discipline in expressing strong emotions
   - Avoids needless conversation
   - Is comfortable with long pauses and silence

For Example

Confucian beliefs have served to shape the Asian culture. A Confucian proverb states, "Those who speak, do not know. Those who know, do not speak." Such information helps us understand the Asian's affinity for and comfort with **silence**.

5. Belief in fatalism
   - Views time as somewhat fluid and flexible
   - Accepts adversity with equanimity

For Example

Asian American Michael Chen lost 95 percent of his shrimp stock (representing US$2.1 million in lost profit) to the Taura virus in 1995. Based in Arroyo City, Texas, Southern Star, Inc., employs thirty-one people and is valued at US$11 million.

The view he expressed was typical of the **fatalism** prevalent in his native Taiwan and in most Asian cultures. In a news report, Chen noted, "It was beyond our control." (*USA Today*, July 5, 1995)

These core beliefs naturally affect the Asian businessperson's **attitude about you** as a EuroAmerican. They may expect you to be:

- Impatient (rushing to "close the deal")
- Talkative or loud (raising voice or interrupting to make points or disagree)
- Too personal (asking embarrassing questions too early in the relationship)
- Self-centered (emphasizing the expertise of self or company)

We all have prejudices. Knowing at the outset what others may think of us is simply one tool we have in designing a successful message. If you are rooted in the European culture, conduct yourself in such a way that you may prove their prejudices incorrect.

To communicate effectively, we need to prepare by accepting advice and making changes that might not be necessary within our own culture.

In preparing to communicate effectively with Chinese officials, American women traveling to Beijing for the International Women's Conference in August 1995, struggled with logistical, political, and cross-cultural problems. They received the following suggestions designed to smooth the way:

- Take only one Bible or holy book since evangelism is prohibited.
- Label your laptop computer as personal property, and do not sell it or allow any Chinese citizen to inspect it, because the government tightly controls technology.
- Dress conservatively by avoiding shorts, sandals, or bright colors.
- Avoid carrying gifts or stacks of brochures through customs.

What is their **attitude about your topic**? Ask yourself the following questions:

- Have they ever conducted business with a U.S. firm?
- What attitudes about American quality might they hold?
- Will they be receptive to discussing shared technology with your company?

FOR EXAMPLE

In 1995–1996, businesses ready to invest in the Indian market needed to consider negative **attitudes** toward U.S. corporations brought about by a shift in political power from the long-entrenched Congress Party to the right-wing Bharatiya Janata Party (BJP).

What started as local protests grew into widely held negative attitudes about Enron Corporation's desire to build a power plant in India. There were unsubstantiated reports of kickbacks, which Enron denied to no avail. The consensus among the populace was that Enron was going to make too much money on the deal.

On August 21, 1995, *Business Week* reported, "The recent cancellation of a US$2.9 billion Indian power project was a huge blow to Enron Corporation's global ambitions. It could also mark the beginning of a big shift in Indian politics. Many Indians were delighted to see a big U.S. corporation cut down to size." The article further cited the "visceral distrust of foreign companies that Indian voters have felt since the colonial era."

The conclusion? "Multinationals are going to have to do what Enron didn't—obtain the blessing of the BJP and other strong political groups. Otherwise, they may suffer the same fate."

What is their **attitude about being there** to receive your message?

- Are they reluctant to even meet with you or eager to open a new market?
- Are they distrustful of your motives in wanting to meet?
- Do they expect to have trouble understanding your accent or idioms?

FOR EXAMPLE

We tend to assume that the rest of the world speaks and conducts business in English, whereas others with whom we try to communicate may have the **attitude** that they don't need to be able to speak English.

Personnel managers of Hong Kong Telecommunications Ltd. report "blank stares" from applicants during interviews conducted in English. One reason is that many students believe when Hong Kong returns to Chinese rule in 1997, the official language will again be Cantonese.

A second reason is that in the education system, teachers now speak Cantonese rather than English, which limits young people's exposure to English. The giant telecommunications firm has therefore increased enrollment in its English classes to 6,000 employees, nearly one-third its workforce.

The impact of such attitudes on U.S. businesses attempting to communicate in English will soon be obvious. (*The Wall Street Journal*, June 9, 1995)

Taking the requisite time to establish a relationship with your primary audience will also help you better understand what the Asian audience **wants to know** about you, your business, your product, or your service. In addition, ask carefully worded questions to discover the information they believe is important.

What an audience **needs to know** in order to make a decision will be guided, at least in part, by culturally influenced attitudes. In purchasing, for example, price and delivery time are paramount for the U.S. business. However, the price or delivery time on a product may be unimportant in relation to overall quality for your Asian customer. Moreover, a high level of quality is a **consistent concern** with most Asian customers. Find out, by asking politely, about other issues that consistently concern them.

FOR EXAMPLE

Any U.S. business that is successful in Japan will have demonstrated a commitment to high quality. GNB Technologies is one such company.

President and CEO Graham Spurling says that GNB is the only non-Japanese supplier to Nippon Telegraph and Telephone (NTT) and overall holds a 10 percent market share.

Other businesses, hopeful of matching GNB's success, might wonder exactly what is meant by a commitment to high quality. Spurling explains, "Our industrial batteries are designed to withstand the shock, vibration, and electro-magnetic effects of a nuclear bomb blast without loss of performance."

Proof of this statement came when disaster struck Kobe, Japan, in February 1995. Industrial batteries supplied by GNB Technologies continued to work, while thousands of backup batteries made by other manufacturers failed and shut down 250 million phone lines in the port city for 24 hours.

Because GNB understands and satisfies the Japanese **concern** for quality, Spurling predicts a 10 percent sales expansion for the next fiscal year. (*Atlanta Journal and Constitution*, April 11, 1995)

ANALYZE YOUR SITUATION

Identify and define the problem.   What set of circumstances require you to communicate with an Asian individual or firm? Are there financial or staffing or production concerns? Do purchasing and shipping schedules create problems? Is the board of directors advocating a change of direction for the company? Or are you concerned about the quality of communication involving your own employees with roots in the Asian culture? Specify the parameters of the problem to reduce the situation to manageable proportions.

FOR EXAMPLE

Procter & Gamble started an ambitious program to export consumer products to China in 1988. Their **problem** was twofold: (1) how to create awareness and trust of a foreign product and (2) how to get the shampoo or detergent into the hands of the Chinese consumer.

Extensive advertising called attention to the problem of dandruff in dark-haired Chinese people and offered *Head and Shoulders* shampoo as a solution. Even though consumers paid a 300 percent premium over local products, the brand proved successful.

What's more, P&G provided a sample size of *Tide* detergent, which was distributed by leaders in "neighborhood committees." That way, the wary Chinese consumers were able to try out the product before buying the larger size.

By taking the time to **identify and define the problem**, Procter & Gamble succeeds where others fail. In 1995, the company projected a profit of $450 million. (*The Wall Street Journal*, September 12, 1995)

Evaluate the corporate culture of the Asian firm.   The Asian business culture is more collectivist than the typical U.S. organization. Among others, two commonly used catch phrases emphasize the difference between an individualistic society and one that is more collectivist.

The EuroAmerican might say, "We're looking out for number one." But the Japanese or Japanese American might answer, "The nail that sticks up will be hammered down." Because of the guiding belief in collectivism, Asian business-people will rarely make decisions unilaterally. Instead, their team or group will evaluate, discuss, and arrive at a decision together.

Even though the Asian culture is collectivist, the organization of each corporation is highly stratified. The structure of an Asian company defines each individual's position in a vertical hierarchy. Each person with whom you communicate will know his or her position relative to every other member of the organization. Such information is essential since it is improper for a person to attempt to interact with someone considered higher or lower in rank.

FOR EXAMPLE

In 1995, Bruce Howard, Manager of Kleen-Tex Industries, Inc., traveled to Japan to learn more about the **corporate culture** of the plant that the company had opened in 1980. He observed:

> I found Kleen-Tex Japan to be a company very different from the founding operation. Working for a Japanese company can be a real lesson in formality and discipline.
>
> Japanese manufacturing companies strive to give customers the best quality product possible at the highest attainable efficiencies. Due to the rigidity of company doctrine, my experience there was often quite frustrating. Americans like to show their independence, but the Japanese are brought up to work together.
>
> The hierarchy of the company was well defined and always maintained. There was rarely any open disagreement or in-fighting, especially between the different levels of management. Rather, the dedication to the company was paramount, and insubordination or shirking of one's duties were practically unheard of.
>
> Overall, my time working in Japan was quite positive and educational.

(Excerpted from *Yutori*, the newsletter of JETRO, the Japan External Trade Organization, April 1995)

 High-ranking women remain a minority when it comes to business in most Asian countries. For example, in Japan only 1 percent of working women hold managerial positions, and only 14 percent hold professional or technical jobs.

Japanese career women work among crowds of "office ladies" who wear identical uniforms, answer phones, greet visitors, operate elevators, and serve tea, generally until they marry and leave the company. Economist Tomoko Fujii described the men she works with at a Japanese brokerage firm: "Their corporate life is just an extension of their private life. They are using women as tools at home and doing the same at the office. It's not easy to change them."

Experts expect these situations affecting **corporate culture** to change gradually over the next few generations. (*The The Wall Street Journal*, July 26, 1995)

In addition, Asian corporate cultures reflect the basic Asian cultural value of harmony that comes from loyalty, cooperation, and obedience. The Asian business strives for growth to benefit the employees, stockholders, and the national good, unlike U.S. businesses that strive for growth primarily to benefit the stockholders and customers.

FOR EXAMPLE

As we reported earlier, when a shrimp virus threatened to wipe out Michael Chen's Texas-based fishery, Southern Star, Inc., his comment to the press was typical of the Asian culture: "We have to keep this farm going. We have a social responsibility to our employees to provide for their livelihood."

Although Chen's losses totaled US$2.1 million, he will continue operating and planned to raise the less profitable but easier-to-grow red fish in 1996. (*USA Today*, July 5, 1995)

Corporations in Asia tend to dislike legal contracts, or if employed, view them differently than we do in the United States. By definition, a contract suggests an adversarial relationship, which Asians believe may negatively affect group harmony. In addition, Asian managers and executives do not believe that every situation and possibility can be addressed by a contractual document, and they fully expect changes in agreements as conditions evolve.

All these characteristics to a greater or lesser extent may apply to your colleagues, clients, and customers in the United States who have roots in the Asian culture. Understanding the culture can help you identify and avoid possible miscommunications.

In summary, remember these points about the corporate culture of the traditional Asian business:

- Communication takes place horizontally.
- Decisions are based on the benefit to the group.
- Harmony is an important aspect of business.
- The company strives for growth to benefit employees.
- Contracts and litigation are believed to interfere with harmony.

Third, assess the external climate. The business news sections of your local paper can be an excellent source of information about the external climate of the Asian-American business community. In addition, read industry-specific journals and attend conferences and conventions whenever possible to keep up with trends and forecasts for business in the United States.

If you seek to do business with firms in Asia, your task will be more complicated. However, many resources are available to help you become aware of what is going on in the specific industry, related industries, and the Asian government. Take time to carry out the following suggestions:

1. **Consult your business library's online research** services to find information related to your opportunity to communicate. Another excellent source is the *Asian Yearbook*, which supplies information and statistics on thirty-one Asian countries.

2. **Contact colleagues** who have recently conducted business in the Asian country you have selected. Try to get as much general information as possible concerning the external climate.

3. **Call your local Chamber of Commerce** for information about organizations designed to help American businesses succeed abroad.

4. **Consider information about the Asian government.** You may be able to find English-language newspapers published in the particular Asian country you are investigating. There is a close link between the government and even privately owned businesses in most Asian countries.

FOR EXAMPLE

Family connections have always been important in China, but never more so than today. With decentralization of **government** control and growing economic opportunities, power in China is being diffused from the one-leader model. As the nation prospers, so do the children of the revolutionaries who founded the Communist Party.

Forming business clubs and loose family-based alliances, these "clans" look similar to the Latin American–style oligarchy of powerful families. To solidify their power and privilege, China's clans also quietly seek high party, government, and military posts. (*The Wall Street Journal*, July 17, 1995)

---

5. **Contact your local university** for names of professors or foreign exchange students in the M.B.A. program who can provide information.

6. **Call the embassy of the Asian country** in Washington, D.C., for additional information.

7. **Call the Export Opportunity Hotline** operated by the Small Business Foundation of America at 800-243-7232.

FOR EXAMPLE

If you are planning to do business with the Japanese:

- Call the Chamber of Commerce for information.
- Contact JETRO (Japan External Trade Organization), located in most major cities, for information. Ask to be placed on their mailing list.
- Read *The Japan Times*, a Japanese newspaper written in English.
- Spend time getting to know Japanese expatriots working in American firms.
- Find and interview a Japanese expert at your local university.
- Get to know Japanese exchange students.
- Contact the Japanese Embassy in Washington, D.C., for printed material.
- Consult the latest edition of *The Asian Yearbook* in the reference section of your library.

Follow similar advice for other Asian countries with which you plan to conduct business. Also remember that knowing about their heritage will enhance communications with Asian Americans. We have listed other useful references on the Asian culture at the end of the chapter under "Suggested Readings."

ANALYZE YOUR OBJECTIVES

When considering your **overall goals** and how they relate to the Asian culture, take a moment to reflect on your company's mission statement. The mission statement provides a foundation for your communication and helps define the overall parameters that will frame your message. If you are communicating with an Asian-American customer, colleague, or client, look for phrases in your mission statement that reflect Asian values and include these in your message.

The **specific purpose** of the communication depends both on your needs and on the knowledge level of your Asian audience. The important thing to remember about the Asian businessperson is the length of time it will take to move along the decision-making continuum we discussed in Chapter 1. We recommend that you allow more time to achieve this objective.

FOR EXAMPLE

Michael Hudgins managed the International Business Relations Department for a small Japanese construction company, Kurare Kensetsu. His **specific purpose** was to find a construction company for which Kurare could act as a subcontractor and Kansai (West Japan) representative. Over time, he located such a company, Schal Bovis, Inc., and began to pursue and eventually win contracts.

In the August 1995 issue of *Yutori*, Hudgins reported on his five-year experience in Japan. He calls the Japanese government procurement system "exclusive, rigid, abstruse, and biased heavily toward established, well-connected zenecon companies [large Japanese general contractors]." He described the entire process as "slow, arduous, and ineffably frustrating."

Despite of the slow pace of qualifying for and winning contracts, Hudgins remains optimistic. "Foreign involvement in the future market depends on how willing companies are to play the game as it exists presently, work from the inside to effect further change, and reinforce the progress that has already been made." (Excerpted from *Yutori*, the newsletter of JETRO, the Japan External Trade Organization, August 1995)

Finally, what is your **hidden agenda**, your personal objective for this communication? Your company may be downsizing and moving some operations abroad. Perhaps your expertise with the Asian market or with your Asian-American subordinates will make you far more valuable to the company. Whatever your personal and private concerns might be, make sure this hidden agenda does not rush you through the process of relationship building.

In July 1994, Dr. Chiaki Mukai became the first Japanese female astronaut when she flew a record-setting fifteen-day mission aboard the space shuttle Challenger. A cardiovascular surgeon, Mukai and others on the mission conducted microgravity experiments on goldfish, salamanders, and themselves.

Revealing her **hidden agenda**, Mukai responded to a reporter's question by saying, "Sometimes the women feel that, 'There are no women, so maybe I should not do this.' If I can encourage those people, I am more than happy."

CHOOSE YOUR OPTIONS

An understanding of the audience, situation, and objectives will logically lead you to consider your communication options. We will explore three elements: how to send the message (**medium**), who should send it (**source**), and when it should arrive (**timing**).

MEDIA OPTIONS: HOW SHOULD THE MESSAGE BE SENT?

The first question to ask yourself in choosing whether to write or speak, and in what form, is this: What prior contact have I had with this Asian client or representative of an Asian firm? For example, the "cold call" rarely serves any useful purpose as a media option when dealing with an Asian culture. But perhaps you met someone at a trade show and exchanged business cards with the promise of communicating at a later date. Here are some things to think about as you decide on a first step.

Speaking options.   Consider the following when selecting your speaking options:

- **Grapevine.** Information spread by casual talk or word of mouth can be helpful when you begin your communication with an Asian firm. Use employees who can speak the native language to disseminate information about your company and your objectives in after-hours socializing.

- **Conversation.** Conversation can be more confidential than the grapevine, yet still allow for immediate feedback. After-hours dialogue while socializing with Asians will be essential to future success.

- **Interview.** An interview is less desirable when dealing with your Asian audience, especially in the early stages of relationship building. They may be offended by questions that are too direct or in any way personal. However, you may wish to interview American expatriots as a way of collecting information.

- **Phone call or teleconference.** The immediacy of using the telephone may override some of its potential problems. Consider using a conference call with an interpreter for maximum understanding. (Call your long-distance company for information on obtaining interpreters and setting up a call convenient to both time zones.)

- **Meeting.** If there is any chance of misunderstanding between you and your receiver due to a language barrier, try to arrange a personal meeting. Whether conducted through an interpreter or in English, the meeting is a good choice for those who understand Asian cultural expectations. This holds true whether the meeting occurs in the United States or in the Asian country.

- **Formal presentation.** After you have established a relationship of trust with the Asian group, you may choose to deliver a formal presentation. Remember to put most of your analysis in the written report.

    A form of presentation involves the ceremony, something your Asian audience will both expect and enjoy. Your Asian consultant can help you arrange symbolic gifts or other ceremonial activities to launch or celebrate a business agreement.

For Example

In 1995, Mayor Richard Trice of Suwanee, Georgia, helped celebrate the grand opening of Yokohama Tire Company, led by CEO Eika Yamagata.

Because Suwanee has been designated "Tree City" by the Arbor Day Foundation, participants planted a Japanese red maple tree in honor of the event. Both leaders also took part in a traditional sake **ceremony** by breaking open a wooden sake barrel to invoke good luck for all involved.

Ceremonial gestures assisted all participants in attaining their goal of better communication. (*The Atlanta Journal,* July 19, 1995)

Whatever speaking option you choose, remember that if you need to discuss a controversial topic, especially one that is likely to become confrontational, make sure you do so in private to preserve dignity (face). This is equally true in communicating with Asian-American colleagues.

For Example

An accounting professor at a university in the Midwest is known for being a tyrant when it comes to punctuality. Apparently one of her Nepalese foreign exchange students was unaware that by being late, he might be subjected to a stern lecture in front of the class and a resulting **loss of face**.

The professor, however, had recently read a colleague's research article concerning cross-cultural awareness. She therefore called the student aside after class and gave him the same stern lecture. By dealing with his tardiness in private, she preserved the foreign student's sense of dignity and avoided what might have resulted in future passive-aggressive behavior problems.

For the remainder of the term, the student was punctual, and his work was exceptional. Additionally, the professor reports improved communication and rapport with all of her foreign students since making minor changes to accommodate cultural differences.

Writing options.   Look over the following writing options. The greeting card, letter, fax, e-mail, and memo all present opportunities to establish a pleasant atmosphere and warmth with your Asian or Asian-American audience (see Appendix I).

- **Greeting card.** A good initial media choice would be a simple card. In addition to the printed message of a holiday or greeting, you can add a reference to your first meeting. Such correspondence helps build a bridge to future communication.

- **Letter, fax, or electronic mail.** If you choose to write a letter, use pleasant greetings to begin the process of establishing a trusting relationship. Avoid talking about business except in an indirect or abstract way. Eventually, your letters will begin with pleasantries, then progress to business issues, and end with more small talk. Surprisingly enough, similar rules apply to fax or e-mail messages. Open with pleasant greetings before you discuss business.

- **Memo.** Because the structure of a typical Asian office is less compartmentalized, the office memo is not used as often as it is in the United States. Rather, the Asian businessperson uses the memo to formalize more important communication, which takes place face to face.

- **Report.** When writing a longer report, use marketing and consumer data displayed in charts or graphs. The Asian reader expects to spend time analyzing your proposal and reaching a consensus among the group or team. Avoid a direct style of selling. Remember to use oblique language when referring to the expertise or accomplishments of your company.

SOURCE OPTIONS: WHO SHOULD DELIVER THE MESSAGE?

Who should **deliver your message** to the Asian audience? Remember that perceived credibility is most important, particularly in terms of the sender's rank, education, and experience. The person who actually delivers the message will not be the highest-ranking member of your American group. However, your Asian audience will expect a person of importance or high rank to be there. The presence of the high-ranking individual will raise the credibility of the presenter.

If you are presenting alone, refer frequently to the higher-ranking person in your talk. "The president of our company wants you to know...." Because Asian cultures revere age, your best source option may be a mature businessperson.

In her book, *The International Businesswoman of the '90's,* Marlene Rossman reports that Japanese and other Asian businessmen are much more accepting of *foreign* women in high business positions than they are of their own. Therefore, you may consider selecting a high-ranking U.S. businesswoman to **deliver your message**.

You will need to know the number of English speakers or readers in your audience and the approximate level of their English proficiency. If you feel that your audience will only partially understand English, consider using a translator or interpreter.

FOR EXAMPLE

The Waikele Factory Stores mall in Waipahu, Hawaii, has become a shopping mecca for Japanese tourists since 1992. Sports Authority Manager, Yukio Yukawa, experienced quite a problem. "I was running all over the store answering questions," reported the bilingual Yukawa.

The store has now hired four Japanese assistants whose ability to communicate with Asian customers has translated into even greater profits for the company. If managers had anticipated the need for **translators**, profits might have risen even more quickly. (*The Wall Street Journal*, June 29, 1995)

Most experts in this area advise that you select the interpreter to ensure knowledge of your business goals and greater fluency in relaying your message. Contact the embassy of the country, your local university, or others who have business experience in the Asian country for references. Take time to become acquainted with the interpreter, and make sure that he or she knows the purpose of your communication.

You may also wish to hire a consultant or speechwriter who is an expert on the particular Asian culture. Whoever delivers your message will require many communications with your Asian audience before trust is established and business can be conducted.

FOR EXAMPLE

Companies as diverse as Duracel, Frito-Lay, Pepsico, Singer, and Dunlop/Slazenger have all used the services of Dr. David E. Shaner to help gain market access, market share, and increased profits. Located in Greenville, South Carolina, Shaner and Associates helps U.S. corporations form joint ventures, mergers, strategic alliances, and partnerships.

As Professor of Asian Studies at Furman University and author of two books on Japanese culture, Shaner represents the kind of **consultant** available through colleges and universities.

To summarize, when considering source options remember the following:

- Select a person of relatively high rank to be present.
- Select a mid-ranking person to conduct the presentation.
- Choose a well-educated presenter.

- Choose an older rather than a younger employee.
- Select an interpreter who understands your communication goals.
- Consider hiring an Asian consultant or speechwriter.

TIMING OPTIONS: WHEN SHOULD THE MESSAGE ARRIVE?

Again, consider the needs of your audience in conjunction with your own communication goals to decide **when to send the message**. As a EuroAmerican dealing with an Asian audience, remember that you will be spending twice as much time in setting up the framework for successful communication with them as you would with audiences having roots in the European culture.

Most Asian cultures fall somewhere in between a polychronic and a monochronic time orientation. For more information, see the Comparative Time Orientation Chart in Appendix A.

Instead of making stereotypical cultural assumptions, the careful communicator will analyze a specific audience when selecting **timing options**, as the following examples illustrate:

- The Japanese bullet train always arrives on time, and Japanese businesspeople expect you to be prompt for meetings. However, they tend to blur the distinction between work and leisure, so the "workday" may end very late at a karaoke bar.
- On the Indian continent, workers take a relaxed attitude toward time, except where they may have been heavily influenced by the British culture, which tends to be more monochronic (see Appendix A).

Holidays are important to most cultures. Be aware of the holidays observed by your particular Asian audience, and avoid trying to do business during those times (see Appendix L for a list of national holidays).

In summary, remember the following when considering timing options as they apply to your Asian audience:

- Allow extra time to build trust and conduct negotiations.
- Be on time for every appointment or meeting, even if you expect to wait.
- Space your appointments so that you never appear to be rushed.
- Expect to spend some after-work hours socializing with your Asian audience.
- Try to value the relationship over the schedule.
- Avoid the days before and after holidays.

COLLECT AND ORGANIZE YOUR INFORMATION

 After you have considered the environment and chosen your options, select an appropriate organizational plan for your speech, letter, interview, report, or meeting. As with most other matters, individuals with roots in the Asian culture differ from Americans in their preferences for a particular style of organization. Some specific guidelines to use when communicating with an Asian audience follow:

1. **Consult Appendix D** for basic, flexible organizational plans. In addition, always begin your persuasive message with disclaimers such as, "I hesitate to offer my opinion on such a complex topic."

2. **Limit your information.** Limit your speech to no more than three main points for the Asian audience. You can provide more detailed information in the written report that will follow your oral presentation.

3. **Enhance the written report with visual aids, numbers, and examples**, remembering to convert to metric (see Guidelines for Visual Aids in Appendix F and Sample Visuals in Appendix G). Avoid sports idioms and commonly used metaphors such as, "We will touch base after the first of the year," or "She had egg on her face." Such expressions will not translate effectively.

4. **Use symbolic gestures** to enhance your message.

FOR EXAMPLE

The CEO of South Korea's Cheil Foods and Chemicals, Inc., Lee Jai Hyon, met with DreamWorks visionary, David Geffen, to discuss a possible investment deal.

Mr. Lee mentioned Cheil's agreement with Quaker Oats Co. to license Snapple. Geffen later offered Lee a cold bottle of Snapple. An executive familiar with the meeting remarked, "At that point, we knew they were hitting it off."

The bottle of Snapple **symbolized** a successful business agreement between a U.S. firm and Cheil, something Geffen hoped to duplicate. (*The Wall Street Journal,* July 18, 1995)

---

5. **Tailor your message to your specific Asian audience** by following these guidelines:

   • **Use short sentences and plain words.** Remember to use one-word verbs whenever possible for easier translating.

   • **Use humor carefully** being sure to employ the services of a consultant from the specific Asian country where you are doing business. Asian audiences appreciate humor, but it must originate from their specific culture, not yours.

   • **Focus on issues relating to the entire group.** Never single out an individual for praise or other comment. For example, thank the entire group for making your travel arrangements rather than the individual who was responsible.

- **Avoid bragging or being too assertive.** Carefully word messages about your company's expertise, and avoid discussing your individual expertise. In other words, be modest and think collectively.

CrossTalk YOUR MESSAGE, ORAL OR WRITTEN

Now that you are armed with well-selected, organized, and supported information, you may **CrossTalk** that information by means of your chosen medium to your Asian audience. When we say **CrossTalk** your message, we are referring to the accommodations you will need to make to better communicate with an audience from a different culture.

ORAL MESSAGES

Remember that in the EuroAmerican culture, we focus on eloquent speech to communicate our messages. Businesspeople rooted in the Asian culture may distrust words and rely more heavily on nonverbal communication. If nonverbal language in the EuroAmerican culture makes up 80 percent of our communication, you can assume that for most Asian cultures, the nonverbal percentage is closer to 90 percent.

For a country such as the United States or Switzerland, a successful presentation will exhibit high energy and rhetoric. Conversely, most businesspeople rooted in the Asian culture prefer calm talk, small gestures, and many niceties.

Some of our confusion arises because many well-educated Asian businesspeople speak English. We assume, therefore, that we "speak the same language." In truth, when a Japanese or Korean businessperson speaks English, the cultural forms and values of their native languages may remain.

Unless your Asian counterparts studied in the United States, their English may be more indirect or ambiguous.

FOR EXAMPLE

The summer of 1995 proved difficult for Japanese banking. A *Wall Street Journal* headline announced "Japan's Banking Mess" on July 7.

One month later, Tokyo's largest credit union failed after depositors withdrew $680 million in one day. Just two days before the collapse, the *Mainichi Shimbun*, in typical **indirect** style, had reported "Cosmo Credit Union Self-Rehabilitation Difficult." (*US News & World Report*, August 14, 1995)

As U.S. businesspeople, we would be wise to avoid the following typical behaviors when communicating with an audience with roots in the Asian culture:

- Arguing openly
- Interrupting frequently
- Making bold gestures
- Disclosing negative emotions
- Discussing personal matters
- Referring to people by given names

Additionally, during presentations, EuroAmericans often try to get as close as possible to the audience. We stand only an arm's length away from an individual listener. Such closeness seems most unusual and uncomfortable to an Asian or even an Asian American, and we need to be aware of this potential communication barrier.

If the Asian or Asian American you are addressing begins to back away slightly, do not move forward to close the space. You may feel a bit awkward, but you will help make the communication much more comfortable for your listener.

When you deliver an oral presentation to your Asian audience (an individual or a group), remember these guidelines:

1. **Rehearse** more than you would for an audience of your cultural peers. Use a mirror to make sure you keep your gestures close to the body. Your smaller gestures and more stationary stance will look "natural" only if you are well rehearsed.

2. **Dress appropriately.** Consider the corporate culture in determining appropriate appearance. Asian corporations tend to be quite formal. Your message will be more seriously considered if you mirror the image of the Asian corporation.

FOR EXAMPLE

At a less than successful meeting, Samsung executives wore business suits and ties, whereas DreamWorks executives wore blue jeans. Not surprisingly, the Samsung decision maker stated that, "the timing was not quite right" for an agreement.

Korean businesspeople expect to see appropriate business attire since it demonstrates both respect and knowledge of their cultural preferences. (*The Wall Street Journal*, July 18, 1995)

---

3. **Take time to warm up.** Your pronunciation should be well articulated. If you are using an interpreter, pause frequently and speak slowly. Repeat key points using slightly different vocabulary for maximum understanding. If someone in the audience asks a question, avoid interrupting.

4. **Moderate your voice.** Avoid raising your voice to make an important point. The Asian audience wants to know the speaker, not the speaker's words.

5. **Address the senior members of the team correctly** and in the appropriate order. The most important member of their team may be introduced and acknowledged last rather than first. Ask your consultant.

6. **Show your audience that you care.** Your Asian audience will forgive you if you are not perfect in your presentation. The most important element of your success with your Asian audience will be to show sincere commitment to your message and the careful communication of that message.

In summary, if you are making your oral presentation on Asian soil, the preceding suggestions are extremely important. If you are communicating with a multicultural group in America, you will probably use the typical EuroAmerican style of speaking.

Be aware, however, that Asian expatriates and others from similar cultures may be initially puzzled, annoyed, or embarrassed by the U.S. platform style. Be prepared to discuss any resulting miscommunications in private. The more you interact with those from the Asian culture, the more you will find yourself adapting to their style, just as they will adapt to yours.

WRITTEN MESSAGES

The following list includes some general advice for writing to an Asian audience (see Appendix I, Sample Letters, Memos, and Faxes):

1. **Complete the Outline Worksheet (Appendix C).** After analyzing your Asian reader, write the most difficult sentences first. These could include initial, final, or bad news sentences. You should also spend extra time in softening any bad news you may need to give the Asian reader.

2. **Use common definitions and active, one-word verbs.** Because your Asian audience may be using a dictionary to assist in translating your letter or other written material, use the most common definition of a word. Also, avoid two-word verbs. "What is your conclusion when you *add up* net returns?" could be rewritten to read, "What is your conclusion when you *calculate* the net returns?"

3. **Avoid idiomatic expressions.** When writing for the Asian audience, strive to write clearly by avoiding slang, jargon, and acronyms.

4. **Keep your sentences and paragraphs short.** Doing so will assist the translator or the Asian who reads English.

5. **Use a single page** for most business communication such as letters, memos, and electronic mail. Use an executive summary to cover longer reports. If your English will be translated into an Asian language, keep in mind that the resulting letter or other written communication will be up to one-third longer.

6. **Use headings and subheadings**, bullet points, graphs, and charts to guide your reader through longer reports.

7. **Read aloud** as part of your preparation. Mistakes such as word omissions, faulty subject–verb agreement, and poor logic will become more obvious when you hear them. Try to imagine yourself as a speaker of another language as you read. Ask yourself, "Is there anything that might be confusing?"

8. **Cross-translate** crucial documents such as contracts. Begin with written English. After the document is translated into the Asian language, ask someone who is bilingual (not the original translator) to translate it back into English. Compare the cross-translation to the original English version for accuracy of key points.

CONFIRM EVALUATION FOR SUCCESS

Feedback

When you are communicating with an Asian audience, you may hear verbal cues that tell you they hear what you are saying. Do not confuse these verbal cues with agreement, however. They may or may not agree with what you are communicating.

FOR EXAMPLE

Robert Goldman's first presentation to a Japanese audience proved to be a difficult and embarrassing lesson in cross-cultural communication. Goldman returned from the initial meeting believing he had "sold" the Japanese company on the idea of swapping optics technology in a joint venture. In fact, he told everyone in his New York office of his success. "I just don't understand what went wrong," he complained after learning his request had been denied.

What Goldman had heard was a repetition of "hai," the Japanese word for "yes," accompanied by a nod of the head. What he didn't understand was that the nodded "hai" during conversation with a Japanese listener means "Yes, I'm trying to follow you." It may or may *not* indicate the listener *agrees* with what you say or even fully understands what you mean.

On his next foray into the international marketplace, Goldman prepared by discussing his audience with an Asian consultant.

Trying to rush through relationship building and on to your message will ultimately backfire. Further, you may not even realize your message is being rejected, because the language used by the Asian counterpart may not specify a negative answer even when one is intended. Remember that people with roots in the Asian culture value harmony, and they will strive to maintain it even when faced with bad news.

FOR EXAMPLE

The summer of 1995 marked difficult times for the United States and Japan. *The Wall Street Journal*, in a June 12, 1995, article, reported the "worst deterioration of US–Japan ties in 50 years" because of the dispute over automobile imports.

At about the same time President Bill Clinton was threatening to impose $5.9 billion in tariffs on Japanese luxury cars, Prime Minister Tomiichi Murayama claimed, "I do not have the view that Japan–U.S. relations are deteriorating. We are enjoying good relations."

The prime minister's words were intended to preserve at least the appearance of harmony in the relationship between the two economic powers.

Asian businesspeople will not answer a direct request negatively. To do so would be rude in their culture. Signs that your Asian audience may not be in agreement with your statements will be subtle. Be alert for the following clues that may signal a negative response:

- Changing the subject
- Apologizing
- Asking a question
- Requesting more information
- Giving a vague answer
- Silence (may be positive or negative)

Also try to understand what may seem to be inappropriate giggles or laughter. These may signal confusion or embarrassment rather than a reaction to something humorous. If your audience laughs at what would be considered inappropriate times in the U.S. culture, you might try again to convey your message.

The best way to judge whether you have been successful is to participate in after-hours socializing. When everyone relaxes, the conversation will reveal the true nature of your success or relative failure. Through socializing, you will also become more accustomed to the nonverbal nature of much of Asian communication.

When evaluating feedback from an Asian audience:

1. **Listen carefully to comments.** We all have natural tendencies to want to defend ourselves against criticism, but thoughtful silence is the most appropriate response in dealing with individuals from the Asian culture.

2. **Do not expect praise.** Even if your Asian audience is pleased with your oral presentation and written report, do not expect individual praise. Giving an individual praise may destroy group unity in the eyes of the Asian colleague, customer, or client. Praise, if given, will probably be directed to your entire group or company.

3. **Paraphrase to confirm meaning.** Your perceptions may not be consistent with your evaluator's intentions. Politely ask for examples, and try the phrase, "Please tell me more." Allow much more time for response than with a EuroAmerican colleague, customer, or client. Allow time for silence.

4. **Correct in the *direction* of the evaluation.** In other words, do not overreact. Your Asian audience will accept your relative inexperience in dealing with their culture if you offer accommodations that will move you toward an agreement.

5. **Accept responsibility.** Avoid the tendency to offer reasons or justification for any proposals or actions that generate concern. An Asian audience prefers an apology as a way to preserve harmony. Your Asian audience will appreciate every gesture you make to preserve dignity (face).

FOR EXAMPLE

- During the U.S.–Japanese auto trade dispute in the summer of 1995, the deputy head of the U.S. trade mission in Japan, adapting to the Asian style of communication, "expressed regret that Japan's unwillingness to open its market in this sector had led the U.S. Trade Representative (Mickey Kantor) to announce these possible measures." (*The Wall Street Journal*, June 13, 1995)

- The General Manager of Daiwa Bank in Japan spoke to the media after discovering the loss of US$1.1 billion by a New York bond trader. Masahiro Tsuda said, "We are deeply embarrassed." He and other top Daiwa officers—in a gesture accepting **responsibility**—will take 10 percent to 30 percent pay cuts for six months. (*USA Today*, September 29, 1995)

---

6. **Look for it in writing.** Your Asian colleague, customer, or client will be more likely to communicate true objectives and concerns in writing than by speaking. Look closely for subtle differences in what you have proposed and what the Asian businessperson has offered in writing.

 Expect some differences in the actual language of Asian men and women. Grammatical structures of the women, particularly verb forms and vocabulary, tend to be even more polite than those of the men.

You may have to ask leading questions and then listen carefully to learn of your female Asian audience's criticisms or concerns.

CREDIBILITY

Our ultimate objective, of course, is credibility. Building credibility with your Asian colleagues, clients, or customers will take time. Your knowledge of their expectations is the most effective and efficient tool you can employ. (Refer to the Kenton Credibility Model on page 19 in Chapter 1.)

- Maintain a sense of group harmony while preserving the dignity of the individual. By doing so, you will achieve the perception of **goodwill**.
- Reveal information about your education and university affiliation either in written form or informally in after-hours socializing with your Asian audience to achieve the perception of **expertise**.
- Achieve the perception of **power** by subtly and indirectly establishing your high rank and tenure in your corporate hierarchy.
- Control the expressions of self-confidence that are valued in the United States and present a humble style that credits the group, and you will achieve the perception of effective **self-presentation**.

IN CONCLUSION

Any communication expert will agree that doing business between high and low context cultures presents tremendous challenges. However, you are now armed with information which will enable you to overcome potential problems and communicate smoothly and effectively with audiences whose roots are in the Asian culture.

Trust words behind words and reason behind reason.

JAPANESE PROVERB

Suggested Readings on the Asian Culture

Carr-Ruffino, N. *Managing Cultural Differences*. Cincinnati, OH: Thomson Executive Press, 1995.

Catlin, Linda, and White, Thomas. *International Business: Cultural Sourcebook and Case Studies*. Cincinnati, OH: SouthWestern, 1994.

Goldman, Alan. *Doing Business with the Japanese: A Guide to Successful Communication, Management, and Diplomacy*. Albany, New York: State University of New York Press, 1994.

O'Hara-Devereaux, Mary, and Johansen, Robert. *Globalwork: Bridging Distance, Culture, and Time*. San Francisco: Jossey-Bass, 1994.

Rossman, Marlene. *International Business Woman of the 90's*. New York: Praeger Press, 1990.

Terpstra, Vern, and David, Kenneth. *The Cultural Environment of International Business*. Cincinnati, OH: SouthWestern, 1991.

Victor, David. *International Business Communication*. New York: Harper Collins, 1992.

CHAPTER 5

WHAT IF YOUR AUDIENCE HAS ROOTS IN THE LATINO CULTURE?

On creating cultural links across borders:

Brazilians living in Miami can now read São Paulo's daily newspaper, beamed by satellite to a computerized press a few miles away, watch Brazilian television via satellite, send and receive facsimile messages within seconds, telephone Brazil at the touch of a finger, and fly there frequently to visit family and friends.

THE WORK OF NATIONS BY ROBERT B. REICH, SECRETARY OF LABOR

As technology speeds our progress into a truly global society, we may lose sight of the differences between our culture and the cultures of people whose homelands touch our borders. However, we must be aware of these differences to effectively communicate our messages.

In this chapter, we examine general cultural characteristics of individuals from Mexico, Central America, South America, and the Caribbean. We also have included the Philippines because in our analysis of that culture, we find it to be quite similar to other, more traditionally classified, Latino countries. We will also discuss Latino Americans who continue to be influenced by their ethnic culture.

Collectively, Latin American countries represent a huge consumer market. Experts predict this market will exceed that of either Europe or Japan by the year 2000, numbering in excess of 400 million people.

Between 1990 and 1994, U.S. Census data shows the Latino-American (Hispanic) population moved closer to becoming the nation's largest minority group with a 16 percent increase from 22,354 million to 26,077 million. Census officials project an increase of up to 50 million by the year 2020. Thus, understanding their cultural roots will help U.S. businesses operate more efficiently and with greater internal harmony.

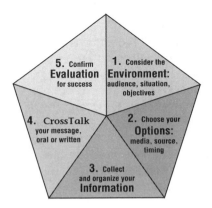

CONSIDER THE ENVIRONMENT

If you have worked through the first four chapters, you are familiar with step one of the **CrossTalk** Communication Model, consider the environment: audience, situation, and objectives. In the relationship-oriented Latino society, understanding your audience will carry the utmost importance.

ANALYZE YOUR AUDIENCE

Latin America includes fifty-one countries. From country to country, vast differences exist in the ways of doing business. Even within certain countries, two cities may be as diverse as New York and Los Angeles.

We will highlight differences between cities or countries within the greater culture within boxes marked with an icon which denotes "Intracultural Notes."

Identify all potential audiences: primary, hidden, and decision makers.   Your primary audience will be a contact person you identify with the help of one of the agencies we have listed under "Assess the external climate" on pages 105–107. The primary audience is the actual individual to whom you speak or write.

FOR EXAMPLE

In Mexico, you would write a letter to the *director de negocios internacionales* and follow up with a phone call. After building a relationship with the **primary audience** over time, you will be ready to fly to Mexico City for a meeting. (Do not expect to conduct business at this initial meeting, however.)

Your hidden audience will probably be a senior officer of the Latino company. As you build a relationship with your primary audience, you will be introduced to the senior official with whom negotiations can take place over time.

The decision maker will usually be that same senior official. Your reputation and that of your company, your status, and the relationship you have built over time will be of utmost importance to the Latino decision maker. In fact, as you study the people from the countries of Latin America, you will see a common theme emerge. In all these countries, mutual relationships between business "friends" hold extremely high priorities for decision makers. The pattern of doing business based on relationships can also be seen in businesses owned by Latino Americans.

FOR EXAMPLE

Ford executive Jorge Di Nucci recognizes an important aspect of dealing with Argentine **decision makers**. "These are amazing markets. Right now we have to invest a lot *to serve them* but we think we can make money [over time]." (Emphasis added.) Ford reported that automobile sales rose 29 percent in 1994 in Argentina. (*The Wall Street Journal*, June 23, 1995)

Investigate and learn about each audience.   After you have identified your audience, try to learn **facts** about them that will help you understand their **attitudes**, **wants**, and **concerns**.

First, consider these **facts** about the Latino culture that affect communication. Think of these facts as core beliefs or values. Individuals with roots in the Latino culture may tend to:

1. Value family and loyalty to family

2. Honor nationalism

3. Exhibit a strong sense of honor

4. Possess a fatalistic view of the world

5. Express passion in speech, manner, and deed

As a result of these core beliefs and values, we can expect the following communication **attitudes** and **behaviors**:

1. Because individuals from the Latino culture value family, they may:
   - Sacrifice for the good of the family, yet remain fiercely independent
   - Show responsibility for family members throughout life

FOR EXAMPLE

It is September 1995, and Anahuac, Mexico, a town of 25,000, is in crisis. The town's bank and a paper mill have closed. Drought has killed 300,000 cattle in the surrounding Chihuahua state. Hundreds of acres of farmland remain unplanted. Double-digit inflation has effectively decimated the income of those who still manage to hold jobs.

But thanks to the strength of the **family**, Anahuac is also a stable town. Resident Roberto Dominquez says his two sons (as well as most of the town's young adults) now work in Phoenix, Arizona, so they can send much needed U.S. dollars home. Other families have moved in together to save housing costs. And many have jointly decided to feed the family rather than keep their cattle alive.

Until better times arrive, Anahuac will remain a symbol of the strength and determination of a culture strongly centered on the extended family unit. (*The Wall Street Journal*, September 7, 1995)

   - Live with the extended family
   - Believe what is good for the family or group is good for the individual
   - Establish a bond with the individual representative of a company rather than with the company as a whole
   - Make decisions from the top of the hierarchy

When Corazon Aquino was elected president of the Philippines, she addressed both expectations and biases and reassured her audience that decisions would continue to come from the **top of the hierarchy**. *Time* (Special Edition, Fall 1990) reports her as saying, "I will remain a mother to my children, but I intend to be Chief Executive of this nation. And for the male chauvinists in this audience: I intend as well to be the Commander in Chief of the Armed Forces of the Philippines."

Unlike Aquino, most Latino women do not break with tradition. In the United States, for example, Mexican-American women are more likely to stay home with small children and less likely to go to college than their EuroAmerican counterparts.

2. Because they honor nationalism, they may:
   - Believe the government should provide jobs

- Enjoy international sporting events
- Show pride in their museums and government buildings
- Recognize the beauty of their countryside

3. Because they exhibit a strong sense of honor, they may:
   - Consider honor vital to decision making
   - Exhibit courtesy and dignity in business and family affairs
   - Be loyal to employer or employees

FOR EXAMPLE

Attorney Loida Nicolas Lewis took control of the largest U.S. black-owned company, TLC Beatrice, after her husband, who founded the company, died. In September 1995, the National Foundation for Women Business Owners and *Working Woman Magazine* named her the nation's Top Woman Business Executive.

In her acceptance speech, Lewis demonstrated **loyalty and commitment to her family and her employees**. She credited her husband, her 4,500 employees, and her extended family, both Philippine and African-American, for her success. (Associated Press, October 8, 1995)

4. Because they possess a fatalistic view of the world, they may
   - Have a flexible view of time
   - Wait to see what develops
   - Believe the future is uncertain
   - Live in the moment
   - Avoid uncertainty

FOR EXAMPLE

A colorful figure in the Mexican political arena, Manuel Camacho recently decided to resign from the long-entrenched Institutional Revolutionary Party (PRI) with plans to form a new political coalition, or even a Ross Perot–style political party. He grabbed national attention when he complained openly and bitterly about not being chosen as the PRI's presidential candidate in 1993. (It is considered poor form for losers to complain openly rather than simply disappear from public view.)

Known for his daring, Camacho put his life in peril when he trekked into the jungle at night to negotiate with the rebel Chiapan Indians early in 1995. And he is often seen at stylish, bohemian night clubs. Because he did not fit the traditional political mold, Camacho created a feeling of uneasiness and uncertainty among his peers.

After his PRI departure, the party leader, Santiago Onate, seemed relieved, "Finally, we have a clear answer among all the confusion and ambiguities that have characterized his attitude....**Certainty** is always good." (*The Wall Street Journal*, October 16, 1995)

5. Because they express passion in speech, manner, and deed, they may:

- Make decisions based on general principles of agreement
- Be impatient with documentation as an obstacle to decision making
- Use power plays or exploit weaknesses in negotiations
- Value emotional sensitivity
- Assert ideas from a highly personal point of view

Latino businessmen tend to be more **assertive** and direct than their female counter-parts. In social situations, male and female communication styles are even more distinct, even exaggerated. Women express more of a nurturing communication style, whereas men express more of an aggressive style.

We offer these core beliefs, attitudes, and behaviors as mere starting points for intercultural awareness. Your specific Latino or Latino-American audience may exhibit widely variable tendencies.

Therefore, in addition to facts about the broad Latino culture, you should gather personal and professional facts about the individuals with whom you are communicating. Include information about age, gender, education, job description and status, university, political party, religious affiliation, and knowledge of your topic. These facts, in turn, influence your audiences' **attitudes** about **you**, about your **topic**, and about actually **being there** to receive your message.

What attitudes might Latino businesspeople have about **you** as a Euro-American businessperson? They may believe you will:

- Take advantage of them if given a chance
- Seem unfriendly because you stand too far away when speaking
- Be obsessed with the future
- Value deadlines over relationships
- Be self-centered or impatient
- Value profit more than people

Knowing at the outset what others may think of us is simply one tool we have in designing a successful message that overcomes biases and negative perceptions.

What is their attitude about your **topic**? Consider these questions:

- Have they ever conducted business with a U.S. firm?
- Does your proposal contradict their core beliefs in any way?
- What misconceptions might they hold about your topic?

Out of courtesy, a Latino audience might not bring up their negative attitudes about your product, industry, or idea. Consequently, determining attitude is extremely important for your future success.

What is their attitude about **being there** to receive your message? Consider these questions:

- Are they reluctant to meet with you?
- Will your timetable interfere with their family obligations?
- Are they somewhat afraid you will embarrass them in some way because of your lack of intercultural awareness?
- Do they expect to conduct business in Spanish?

In Mexico or Argentina, the language of business is English. In many Latin American countries, however, businesspeople will expect to use Spanish to conduct business. Being fluent in Spanish or having a competent translator is extremely important. Knowing even a few Spanish words or phrases can help you gain acceptance.

Portuguese and French are also languages you will find spoken in Latin America. Make sure you know the language of the specific country you plan to visit. Using your few Spanish phrases in Brazil, where people speak Portuguese, would be an unforgivable breach of etiquette.

Determine their wants over your needs.   What any businessperson wants to know in order to make a decision is guided, at least in part, by culturally learned attitudes. If you think back to the core beliefs or values of people from the Latino culture, you will understand some of the things they will want to know. For example, they may be interested in whether or not your firm has the same values of loyalty and honor as their own. They may want to know that your timetable is somewhat flexible. And they may be interested to know if your commitment to them is merely for short-term profit or for a long-term relationship.

FOR EXAMPLE

In 1995, consumer products giant Procter & Gamble Co. announced investments of $US100 million in Mexico and Brazil. P&G Latin America chief, Jorge Montoya, stated, "We're not putting that kind of money in for [returns on investments in] the next six months. We're talking 20, 30 years." Such **long-term** planning makes good economic sense when doing business with the Latino culture. (*The Wall Street Journal*, June 23, 1995)

Long-term relationships, loyalty to the country, and emotional benefits are important to this audience. Find out, by asking politely, about other issues that consistently concern them. The longer you work with your Latino or Latino-

American colleague or client, the more easily you will recognize individual concerns. You may expect, however, that these concerns will reflect family, honor, and nationalism.

ANALYZE YOUR SITUATION

Identify and define the problem.   At this step in your communication process, reflect on the decision that made it necessary to write or speak. For example:

- Do you want to take advantage of Panama's tax-haven status or Mexico's abundant labor supply?
- Are you concerned that the morale of your Latino-American employees in your Houston branch may be negatively affected by the urgent tone of your recent communication?
- Do you want to sell cosmetics in Brazil but have no idea how to deliver them to remote areas?

Avon faced a daunting **problem** when it decided to expand into the vast market of Latin America. How would they be able to make their product available in remote areas where the lack of good roads and bridges makes transportation a veritable nightmare?

James Brooke reported Avon's solution in a *New York Times* article titled, "Avon is calling in Brazil." Using the person-to-person strategy that has worked so well for them in the United States, Avon employs a part-time salesforce of 478,000 women. According to Brooke, Avon's female troops more than double that of the Brazilian army. And where other modes of transportation are not available, these "cosmetics commandos" deliver products on foot.

This incredible networking business of women selling to women has made Brazil the company's largest market outside the United States. (*The New York Times*, July 6, 1995)

Asking yourself such questions will help you define the problem and better focus your message. Failure to carefully define the problem will result in a lack of direction and possible loss of opportunity.

Evaluate the corporate culture of the Latino firm.   When considering the corporate culture of any Latino business, you should examine at least four issues:

1. Patriarchal hierarchy
2. Polychronic time orientation
3. Developing technology and infrastructure
4. View of legal contracts

First, people from the Latino culture are very concerned with the well-being of the extended family. Such an attitude carries over into businesses where workers up and down the hierarchy develop loyalty to a patriarch. Because of loyalty to family and the patriarch, a Latino or Latino-American businessperson may favor friends or family above expertise or experience in making corporate decisions. In addition, you will find few women in executive positions, a situation that will change gradually over the next few generations.

The following examples highlight the effects of a **patriarchal culture**:

- In Brazil, only 36 percent of women work, and more than half of these do home-based piece work.
- In Mexico, few executive positions are available for women, according to Maria Elena Juarez, a partner in the executive search firm Amrop International. She says that some multinational companies are receptive to interviewing a woman for an executive position. However, when Mexican companies describe their requirements for a candidate, it is often apparent they are describing a man. (*The Wall Street Journal*, June 26, 1995)

Second, because the Latino culture has a polychronic time orientation, issues relating to time will receive less attention than issues relating to people or relationships. Polychronic cultures view time as flexible and fluid rather than as a commodity to be spent, saved, budgeted, or lost (see Comparative Time Orientation Chart in Appendix A).

FOR EXAMPLE

Your appointment **time** is approximate, so do not take it personally if you have to wait. During your meeting, you may be invited to lunch. The leisurely two-hour lunches provide an opportunity to establish friendship and better assess the corporate culture rather than a time to discuss business. Remember that the office day ends late, so there will be plenty of time to discuss more specific issues later.

Third, businesses located in small towns or rural areas in Mexico, Central or South America, or the Caribbean rely less heavily on technology than their U.S. counterparts. Electricity and telephone services are still developing in all but the largest cities. In addition, infrastructures are failing in many locations, which makes transportation less reliable. The weak infrastructure may contribute to the slower pace of business in Latino countries.

Consider these contrasts in communication **technology** in two Latin American countries, Mexico and Brazil:

Before becoming privatized in a hugely successful stock offering, Mexico's state-owned telephone system, Telmex, was in a shambles. With investments of US$2.5 billion per year, satellites, fiber optics, and cellular phones have become more prevalent, with impressive communications results.

However, Motorola Inc.'s country manager, Flavio Grynszpan, believes Brazil's telephone monopoly, Telecomunicacoes Brasileiras SA, is still a long way from becoming privatized. Consequently, foreign investors should rely less heavily on the assurance of rapid communication when developing their plans to do business in Brazil.

Finally, just as in the United States, Latino businesses employ litigation to solve many disputes. However, they may view contracts differently. Corporations in Latino businesses will use legal contracts but may expect to continually renegotiate after signing. Consequently, the pace of negotiation tends to be much more relaxed than in the United States.

Understanding these four issues—patriarchal hierarchy, polychronic time orientation, developing technology and infrastructure, and view of legal contracts—will help you move to the next step in the **CrossTalk** Communication Model: assessing the external climate.

Assess the external climate.   Many journals and newspapers deal with specific topics relevant to your particular industry. Additionally, business news is becoming a greater part of television news programming. Utilize these resources to become familiar with the external climate of the industry with which you will be communicating in the United States. You will discover industry trends and forecasts by attending conventions, as well.

If you seek to communicate with businesses located in Latino countries, you can become aware of specific industry trends as well as government regulations and progress toward privatization by consulting the following:

1. **Your business library's online research services.** Among other references listed at the end of this chapter, look for *Doing Business in Latin America and the Caribbean* by Lawrence W. Tuller (Amacom, 1993). This book provides a useful appendix, which includes information on commercial service offices, export credit insurers, trade promotion organizations, and more.

FOR EXAMPLE

Another excellent resource is *Latin Trade: Your Business Source for Latin America*, published monthly by Freedom Communications, Inc., of Miami (305-358-8373).

2. **The Chamber of Commerce in your area.** Find information about organizations designed to help American businesses succeed abroad. Also contact the Regional Headquarters of the American Chamber of Commerce in São Paulo, Brazil, for information about the American Chamber of Commerce in the Latin American country you have selected.

3. **Colleagues who have recently conducted business in the Latino country.** Try to get as much information as possible concerning the business climate for your particular venture.

4. **English-language newspapers or newsletters.** Collect information about the government of the particular Latino country you are considering. Try to discern the stability of the government. Keep in mind, however, that in some Latino countries, the government controls the media.

FOR EXAMPLE

Businesses wishing to invest in Mexico will find valuable information in the English-language **newsletter** *Inter-American Trade and Investment Law*, published by the nonprofit National Law Center for Inter-American Free Trade in Tucson, Arizona (800-529-3463). The newsletter provides translations of new laws, procurement information, and explanations of how new laws affect trade. Ask about online features that provide additional information on tax codes, banking law, and financial reporting requirements.

---

5. **Your local university.** Ask for names of professors or foreign exchange students in the M.B.A. program who would be willing to provide information on a particular country. (They are also a good source for interpreters.)

6. **The embassy** of the Latino country in Washington, D.C. Ask what information and business services they may provide.

7. **The Export-Import Bank of the United States (Eximbank).** Find information on financing exports by calling 202-565-3946.

FOR EXAMPLE

When a U.S. consortium led by Raytheon Corporation wanted to build a ground and airborne satellite sensing and imaging network for Brazil, they had to find a bank willing to loan them $1.4 billion. Many U.S. banks refuse to consider such loans going out of the United States. Raytheon secured the financing through the **U.S. Export-Import Bank (Eximbank)** located in Washington, D.C.

The Amazon Surveillance System, which will help Brazil protect the region's environment and indigenous people, will create 20,000 jobs and reach completion by the year 2002.

8. **The U.S. Department of Commerce International Trade Administration** (800-USA-TRADE). Ask for the division that specializes in the types of goods or services you represent.

FOR EXAMPLE

If you are planning to conduct business in Mexico:

- Call the U.S. Department of Commerce Trade Development Office.
- Contact the Trade Commission of Mexico in the city closest to you: Chicago, Dallas, Beverly Hills, Atlanta, Los Angeles, New York, or Washington, D.C.
- Call the Mexican-American Chamber of Commerce in Los Angeles, New York, or Washington, D.C.
- Spend time getting to know Mexicans working in American firms.
- Find and interview a Mexican expert at your local university.
- Get to know Mexican exchange students.
- Learn basic Spanish as a courtesy and to help with travel.

Follow similar advice for other Latino countries with which you may wish to conduct business.

ANALYZE YOUR OBJECTIVES

Following the **CrossTalk** Communication Model, you will next consider your objectives and how feasible they are within the Latino culture. Remember from Chapter 1 that your objectives include an overall goal, the specific purpose of the communication, and a hidden agenda.

Your **overall goal** is influenced by the mission statement of your company. For example, a mission statement focusing on customer development and service might be your impetus to develop a Latin-American market or recruit Latino-American managers for your office in the Southwest.

FOR EXAMPLE

The following excerpt from the **mission statement** of a home nursing care organization will be helpful in attracting workers rooted in the Latino culture.

> We recognize that our employees are individuals with family obligations. We also know that happy employees can best provide for the needs of our clients. We will therefore do all in our power to offer child care, maternity and paternity leave, and adequate health benefits to all employees.

The **specific purpose** of the communication should reflect your analysis of your audience and your own personal needs. For example, you may need to open a new market. Recognize, however, that although Latino markets are open and growing, it will take time to make the necessary connections to actually begin to move products across borders.

Your specific purpose will be to immediately open lines of communication with your target markets, knowing that you may not be able to reach these new markets for some time. We recommend that you double the time you usually allocate for achieving this objective, depending on the particular Latino country's negotiating style. The same advice will apply when moving into a heavily Latino-American market such as Miami or Los Angeles.

Finally, what is your **hidden agenda**, that is, your personal objective for this communication? Perhaps you are fluent in Spanish, Portuguese, or French and hope to use your training to see other countries. If you can develop markets in Latin America, your company will pay you to travel. Although unspoken, such an agenda will obviously guide you in making recommendations at work.

However, the same agenda may make you impatient. Therefore, consider all three—your overall goal, your specific purpose, and your hidden agenda—in order to prepare for the next step of the **CrossTalk** Communication Model.

When a nonprofit healthcare organization began a campaign to distribute condoms in Latin America, they articulated their **specific purpose** as "population control" and targeted that message to men. The campaign was a failure.

After careful evaluation of their audience and situation, the organization refocused the campaign to "reduce disease and improve overall family health and welfare." They targeted that specific purpose to women.

Not only was the new campaign more successful, but the company also achieved its **hidden agenda** of reducing the overall birth rate and therefore improving the lives of many impoverished people.

CHOOSE YOUR OPTIONS

After analyzing your audience, situation, and objectives, you are ready to consider your communication options. Remember that your *receiver's* wants and needs will influence your choices of **medium, source, and timing**.

MEDIA OPTIONS: HOW SHOULD THE MESSAGE BE SENT?

In considering how your message should be sent, ask yourself, "What prior contact have I had with this Latino client or business representative?" Consider what you know about your client or colleague individually as well as what you know about the Latino culture collectively.

The cold call is a poor choice as a media option when dealing with individuals in a high-context Latino culture. Because relationships guide business decisions, you will need introductions. Perhaps you will be introduced by a mutual friend. You exchange business cards with the promise of communicating at a later date. Or perhaps you will be introduced by a consultant or liaison whom your firm has hired for this purpose.

In the U.S. business milieu, consider your choice of media options when communicating with employees or managers whose core beliefs may reflect their native Latino culture. Whatever your situation, once you have progressed to this stage in the model, you will be ready to consider your writing or speaking options.

Speaking options.   Information on your speaking options is essential to succeeding with Latino-American co-workers or when presenting to a Latino firm. Many well-educated Latino businesspeople speak English. We may assume, therefore, that we "speak the same language." Unless educated in the United States, however, the Latino businessperson may use English that is more colorful and somewhat less direct. Therefore, consider the following when selecting your speaking options:

- **Grapevine.** Expatriates who have returned to the United States are good sources for word-of-mouth messages. Ask their assistance in initiating such messages, which will become part of the huge networking systems common to any Latino culture.

- **Conversation.** You will spend much time in face-to-face conversations for optimum relationship building, which also provides immediate feedback.

- **Interview.** An excellent way to get to know your Latino audience is by asking appropriate questions that involve world news, the general business climate, sports, family, and mutual friends. Later topics may involve specific requirements for your proposal. Avoid telephone interviews. Your Latino audience will reveal much more information face to face.

- **Phone call or teleconference.** The immediacy of using the telephone may override some of the potential translation problems. Use the phone to arrange general meeting dates or establish mutual contacts. Do not expect to transact business by phone. Call your long-distance company for information on obtaining interpreters and setting up a time for your call to the Latino country. Remember that telephone service is unreliable in all but the largest cities.

- **Meeting.** Whether conducted through an interpreter or in English, the face-to-face meeting is a good choice for those who understand Latino cultural expectations. This holds true whether the meeting occurs in the United States or in a Latin American country. The meeting is your opportunity to establish trust or continue to develop a relationship with the group as a whole.

- **Formal presentation.** After you have established a relationship of trust with the Latino group, you might choose to do a formal presentation. Use the same presentation techniques you would use in the United States, but be more polite and a bit more formal in addressing your audience. (See more information under "Oral Messages" in Chapter 1).

Whatever speaking option you choose, remember that if you discuss a controversial topic, one that is likely to become confrontational, do so in private to preserve respect. Your high-ranking Latino or Latino-American audience may mentally withdraw if you choose to "tell it like it is."

In summary, if you are making your speech or delivering your oral report in a Latino country, the preceding suggestions will ensure your success. If your Latino audience is part of the U.S. workforce, the same suggestions may apply. Remember to use patience and seek to preserve the dignity and respect of the individual in your spoken interactions.

Writing options.   When considering writing options, consider that the greeting card, letter, fax, e-mail, and memo all present opportunities to establish a pleasant atmosphere and warmth. Thus they are excellent choices for individuals from the Latino culture.

- **Greeting card.** A good initial media choice would be a simple greeting card. In addition to the printed message of a holiday or greeting card, you can add a reference to your first meeting. Such correspondence opens the door for future contact (see Appendix L for a list of Latino national holidays). Keep in mind that some Latino Americans continue to celebrate traditional ethnic holidays.

- **Business card.** Having a business card printed in both English and the language of the Latino country says, "I respect your language and your country." Because the Latino culture values education, include your academic degrees along with your title. And whether traveling or at home, treat business cards with respect. Men should keep them in the vest (not hip) pocket.

- **Letter, fax, or electronic mail.** Always begin with pleasantries. Remember to inquire about the family in a general way. Avoid talking about specific business opportunities. Soon, your letters will begin with niceties, then discuss business, and finally end with more pleasantries. Surprisingly enough, the same rules apply to use of the fax or e-mail. Never use first names. Double-check spelling of names, and make sure you use the acceptable form of address for the specific country (see Appendix I for sample letters for the Latino culture).

- **Memo.** The Latino businessperson usually expects a memo to support communication discussed in person. The memo is not used to introduce a business proposal, however, since this is done face to face.

- **Report.** The Latino or Latino-American decision maker will probably spend time analyzing your report and planning actions that will benefit the business family. Remember that points previously agreed to may come under additional scrutiny.

In summary, remember the needs of the receiver of your message as you prepare to communicate in writing with your Latino or Latino-American audience.

SOURCE OPTIONS: WHO SHOULD DELIVER THE MESSAGE?

Who should deliver your message to the Latino audience? Remember that perceived credibility is most important, particularly in terms of the sender's rank, education, and experience. Your Latino audience will expect a "person of importance" to make final decisions. The presence of a high-ranking individual from your team will raise the credibility of your presenter. This is true for Latino audiences in the United States as well.

Because Latino countries are typically patriarchal, individuals from those cultures may not expect to find a woman as a source option. In some cases, traditional sex roles are so ingrained that a female presenter might be **credible** only to another woman.

In Mexico, for example, the education system tends to segregate men and women with female teachers for the girls and male teachers for the boys. This practice establishes and reinforces the credibility of a same-sex presenter.

However, Latino businessmen tend to treat women with great respect in the tradition of machismo. Therefore, a woman can be a pivotal member of your team. Select her to present somewhat controversial issues, which the Latino businessmen will probably hear politely.

In addition, younger Latino businessmen may be more comfortable than their older colleagues in your choice of a woman to present or send your message. Experts predict this situation will gradually change as industrialization progresses and more companies begin to conduct business outside their home country.

If you are presenting alone, refer frequently to the higher-ranking person in your talk: "The president of our company wants you to know...." Since Latinos and Latino Americans typically revere age, consider choosing a mature person as your source.

In parts of Latin America, business is conducted in Spanish. However, Portuguese is the official language of Brazil, and French is the language of several countries in the Caribbean, so be sure to verify which language is used for conducting business in the country you select.

If you are not fluent in Spanish, select a certified interpreter or translator you know and trust. Obtain names of competent professionals from the embassy of the country, your local university, or others who have business experience in the Latino country. Be certain that your interpreter or translator knows the goals of your communication. You will have an added advantage if the person you select is originally from the Latino country or from the "neighborhood" if you are presenting in Spanish-speaking areas of Miami, South Texas, or Southern California.

FOR EXAMPLE

Priscilla Hayes Padron is a certified **translator** of Spanish with more than ten years of experience. She reports that companies often give translation assignments to a bilingual person who is neither a good translator nor a good writer. The result is poorly translated documents that Padron calls "a secret embarrassment" to the companies involved, because the resulting spelling or grammatical errors are rarely reported.

Padron recommends that businesspeople make sure they are as selective about the credentials of the translator as they are about the qualifications of their technical, public relations, legal, accounting, or sales staffs. "Remember," she says, "the translator's words are making the case for your company, and more than likely you cannot evaluate the final product."

Finally, you may also wish to hire a consultant specializing in the Latino country of your choice. Locating one consultant can produce references to others.

TIMING OPTIONS: WHEN SHOULD THE MESSAGE ARRIVE?

In Mexico, you may hear the phrase, "El reloj anda." Literally translated "The clock walks," this proverb tells much about people from the Latino culture and how they may view time. In the EuroAmerican culture, we say, "Time flies," and believe that "Time is of the essence." But in Latino countries, time is secondary to family and relationships. Such information is helpful in determining **when to send your message**. For a Latino audience, you will be spending more time than usual just setting up the framework for successful communication (see the Comparative Time Orientation Chart in Appendix A).

Understanding the Latino concept of **mañana** (literally "tomorrow") is important in any attempt to communicate effectively. Being with family and friends, especially around holidays, may come before business. Avoid the temptation to judge the Latino's culturally programmed way of prioritizing and integrating life and business events. The Latino's commitment will be made to the *person*, not to a time-defined task as in the EuroAmerican culture. Always keep in mind that individuals within the Latino culture will vary in their approach to time management.

FOR EXAMPLE

Consider these comments from Liliana Roman, Special Assistant to the Director of the Americas Program, a nonprofit think tank in Washington, D.C.:

I recognize that **mañana** does exist at some lower levels of business. However, in my dealings with major Latino businesses, I have found people to be very professional and respectful of deadlines.

As a function of hemispheric integration, the Latin American business community is becoming more like the U.S. every day.

If EuroAmericans anticipate the differences in approach to business, we will be able to be more effective in our scheduling. This knowledge can assist us in making important decisions about the timing of our business communication. (See Appendix L for a list of national holidays, and avoid doing business in the days before, during, and after them.)

FOR EXAMPLE

Mexico celebrates many of the same **holidays** as the United States. However, they also observe the following:

- February 5—Anniversary of the Mexican Constitution
- March 21—Juarez's birthday
- May 1—Labor Day
- May 5—Anniversary of the Battle of Puebla (not observed in Mexico city)
- December 1—Reserved for the President's State of the Union Address
- September 16—Independence Day
- November 2—Day of the Dead
- November 20—Mexican Revolution

Be aware of these holidays, and remember to allow several days before and after each holiday for Mexican businesspeople to spend time with family and friends.

COLLECT AND ORGANIZE YOUR INFORMATION

As with most other matters, individuals with roots in the Latino culture prefer a particular style of letters or other written material. (See Appendix I for specific examples of styles appropriate for the Latino culture.)

1. **Collect information about the country.** Because your Latino audience has a strong sense of nationalism, take time to learn something about the general history of the country, as well as information on its contributions to culture and society at large in your introductory remarks. Incorporate such knowledge into your message.

2. **Plan your introduction, main points, and conclusion** in self-contained units so that when you are interrupted, you will not become confused or appear disorganized.

3. **Limit the amount of information** you cover in the body of your report. Keep in mind that facts and figures are not as important as the business relationship.

4. **Focus on one goal or topic at a time.** With so much to remember about cultural differences, it is best to move deliberately and cover one objective thoroughly.

5. **Enhance both writing and speaking** with visual aids, numbers, and examples, remembering to convert to metric where applicable. Rather than present

problem solving, focus on the advantages of your proposal for the Latino firm since the decision may be based on subjective rather than objective data. With the advice of your consultant, use sports references appropriate to the particular country.

6. **Tailor your message for each audience.** Consider all cultural core beliefs as well as specific information about individuals, and double-check to make sure you have not omitted important references or appropriate pleasantries.

Latino American Yanira Merino, originally from El Salvador, built strong union support in a shrimp packing plant in Los Angeles. She was able to do so by appealing to the worker's cultural **core beliefs**, specifically a spirit of collective action for the benefit of the family. Many workers in the packing plants are low-paid women—recent immigrants with families to help support.

The AFL-CIO has expressed interest in organizing such low-paid workers, a high percentage of whom are women from ethnic minorities. The organization believes women are fervent union backers because they readily see the benefits of collective action. (*The Wall Street Journal*, October 23, 1995)

CrossTalk YOUR MESSAGE, ORAL OR WRITTEN

When we say **CrossTalk** your message, we are referring to the accommodations you will need to make to better communicate with an audience from a different culture.

ORAL MESSAGES

If you are talking to your Latino audience (an individual or a group), here are some guidelines:

1. **Take time to warm up.** Your voice should be clear and pleasant with good articulation for your interpreter or audience. Pause more frequently and speak slowly if your Latino audience speaks English as a second language or if you are using an interpreter.

2. **Pause to look at each listener as you talk.** Direct your comments to the individuals in your Latino audience, not to your interpreter.

3. **Reduce physical barriers**, such as stationary microphones. Your Latino audience will feel comfortable if you are fairly close. Do not back away in one-on-one conversations.

4. **Move naturally.** For your Latino audience, use the same size and style of gestures that are acceptable in the United States. (See Chapter 1 under "**CrossTalk** Your Message, Oral or Written.")

5. **Show your audience that you care.** No individual or group will be more aware of your personal commitment than your Latino audience. You must believe in your message and passionately present it.

6. **Always be yourself**, and strive to make your presentation exciting and dynamic.

WRITTEN MESSAGES

The following list includes some general advice for writing to a Latino audience:

1. **Use the Outline Worksheet (Appendix C).** After analyzing your Latino reader, write the most difficult sentences first. These could include initial, final, or bad news sentences. Keep sentence structure simple.

2. **Write as naturally as you speak.** You can do this by choosing simple language. If your writing will be translated to Spanish, write in English, using the most common definition of a word.

3. **Use a single page** whenever possible for most business communication such as letters, memos, and electronic mail. Use an executive summary to cover longer reports. If your English will be translated into Spanish, Portuguese, or French, keep in mind that the resulting letter or other written communication will be longer.

4. **Avoid idiomatic expressions.** When writing for the Latino audience or your interpreter, strive to write clearly by avoiding slang, jargon, acronyms, and sports metaphors.

5. **In a longer paper, use headings and subheadings**, in addition to bullet points, graphs, and charts, to guide your Latino reader through your information.

6. **Cross-translate** crucial documents such as contracts. Begin with written English. After the document is translated into Spanish, for example, ask a bilingual employee (not the original translator) to translate it back into English. Compare the cross-translation to the original English version for accuracy of key points.

CONFIRM EVALUATION FOR SUCCESS

Practice and improvement are the cornerstones of good communication. The improvement results from your evaluation of feedback you receive from your Latino or Latino-American audiences.

Your Latino audience might be very responsive. But their nods and vocal reassurance may indicate only that they respect you and want you to be happy. They may or may not agree with what you are saying.

Latino businesspeople will probably not answer a direct request negatively. To do so would be rude in their culture. In most cases, they will agree to a deadline and have every intention of meeting it. Factor in births, deaths, birthdays, religious holidays, state holidays, and the weeks before and after such events, and you will find these industrious people will indeed meet your "deadline."

FOR EXAMPLE

A EuroAmerican supplier of ingredients for candy bars ordered peanuts from Cordoba, Argentina. Under the GATT agreement, only a certain quota of Argentine peanuts may be imported into the United States, and the quota had already been 95 percent filled. He urgently contacted the salesman in Buenos Aires who said he would make sure the lots of peanuts were ready "immediately" for inspection. Hearing this, the EuroAmerican businessman promptly dispatched an inspector to pull samples from the lots. When the inspector arrived at the Cordoba plant, he was told the peanuts were not yet shelled, but would be ready tomorrow.

After many phone calls and much distress, the peanuts were still ready "tomorrow." The Argentine salesman's comments reflected the miscommunication which had occurred because of the difference in time orientation between the Argentine and the EuroAmerican cultures. "You said you needed the peanuts immediately, and that's when they were ready. This is really very fast. The entire process usually takes much longer."

When evaluating feedback from a Latino audience:

1. **Ask for more information.** Also nod your head frequently to indicate you are hearing the evaluation as it is being given. Politely ask for examples to clarify your understanding.

2. **Accept responsibility.** If you wish to defend your message, do so in such a way that will preserve a sense of dignity and respect with your Latino audience. To "burn a bridge" of communication with one audience will negatively affect your opportunity to communicate with others. So always maintain self-control.

3. **Correct in the *direction* of the evaluation** given by your Latino or Latino-American audience. Consider the rank of the individual offering the criticism. The higher the rank, the more you may need to adjust your message or your approach.

4. **Look for it in writing.** Your Latino colleague, customer, or client will be more likely to communicate true objectives and concerns in writing than by speaking. Look closely for differences in what you have proposed and what the Latino businessperson has offered in writing.

5. **Recognize that your audience's perceptions define reality.** The feedback you receive is a gift offered from a friend. Remembering this will help you grow as you seek to communicate with this special audience.

6. **Remember to thank your evaluator.** Negative feedback is as difficult to give as to receive. Help maintain your dignity and that of your Latino evaluator by being courteous.

Both Latino men and women will take negative feedback personally. Carefully consult your Audience Analysis Worksheet (Appendix B) and the Bad News Model (Appendix D3) when designing a negative message to this audience.

CREDIBILITY

Building credibility with your Latino or Latino-American colleagues, clients, or customers will take time. Your knowledge of their expectations is the most effective and efficient tool you can employ (refer to the Kenton Credibility Model on page 19 in Chapter 1.)

You will achieve the perception of **goodwill** from your Latino audience by taking enough time to become a friend and colleague.

You will achieve the perception of **expertise** by talking or writing about your past successes with other firms in other situations.

You will achieve the perception of **power** with written and spoken material that refers to your rank. Your business card printed in both languages is an effective tool to establish your rank and education.

You will achieve the perception of effective **self-presentation** by laying the groundwork, knowing the culture, and presenting your message with passion and eloquence. Remember to **CrossTalk** your message for optimum results.

IN CONCLUSION

One good way to judge whether you have been successful with your Latino audience is to look for the time-honored phrase, "Mi casa es su casa." Literally translated "My house is your house," the phrase means much more. Figuratively, it is used to indicate that your Latino audience trusts and accepts you as a business partner.

Suggested Readings on the Latino Culture

Axtell, Roger E. *The Do's and Taboos of International Trade: A Small Business Primer*. New York: Wiley & Sons, 1994.

Carr-Ruffino, N. *Managing Cultural Differences*. Cincinnati, OH: Thomson Executive Press, 1996.

Jessup, Jay M., and Maggie, L. *Doing Business in Mexico*. Rocklin, CA: Prima Publishing, 1993.

Morrison, Terri, and others. *Kiss, Bow or Shake Hands*. Holbrook, MA: Bob Adams, 1994.

Reich, Robert B. *The Work of Nations: Preparing Ourselves for 21st Century Capitalism*. New York: Vintage Books, 1992.

Tuller, Lawrence W. *Doing Business in Latin America and the Caribbean*. New York: American Management Association (AMACOM), 1993.

Varner, Iris, and Beamer, Linda. *Intercultural Communication in the Global Workplace*. Chicago: Irwin, 1995.

Appendix Contents

THE CrossTalk QUICK CHART

CrossTalk QUICK CHART

CULTURE CHARACTERISTICS	EURO-MEN	EURO-WOMEN	AFRICAN	ASIAN	LATINO
Polychronic time orientation*		xx	xx	xxx	xxx
Monochronic time orientation*	xxx	xx			
Individualistic society	xxxxx	xxx	x		
Collectivist society		xx	xxx	xxxxx	xxxx
High context**		xx	xxx	xxxxx	xxx
Low context**	xxxxx	xx			
Authoritarian leadership style			xxx	xxxxx	xxxx
Shared leadership style	xxx	xxxxx			
Family and relationships are valued over work		xxx	xxxxx	xxx	xxxxx
Work is valued over relationships	xxxxx	xx		xxxx	
Fatalistic view of life			xxxx	Varies by religion	xxxx
Self-determination most important	xxxxx	xxx			
Mechanistic view of employees***	xxxxx	xxx			
Humanistic view of employees***			xxx	xxxxx	xxxx
Legalistic approach to business	xxxxx	xxx		x	
Approach to business is through relationships		xxx	xxx	x	xx
Face-saving is important			xx	xxxxx	xxxx
Comfortable with silence				xxxxx	
Uncomfortable with silence	xxxx	xxxxx	xxxx		xxxx
Verbal communication preferred	xxxx	xxxxx	xxxx	x	xxxx
Nonverbal communication preferred	x	x	x	xxxxx	x
Women important in business	xxx	xxxx	x		x
Formality in business attitude and attire			xxxx	xxxxx	xxxx

Key: 5x = highest; 1x = lowest.
* See Comparative Time Orientation Chart.
** See Low/High Context Chart.
*** See Mechanistic/Humanistic View of Employee Chart.

A1: Comparative Time Orientation Chart

Monochronic (Linear) Time Orientation	Polychronic (Circular) Time Orientation
Views time as an entity to be saved, spent, or lost	Views time as fluid, flexible
Completes one task before starting another	Works on multiple tasks before finishing any one
Focuses on the task to be completed within a certain time frame	Focuses on and nurtures the relationships represented by the tasks
Separates work from family and social life	Views work, family, and social life as one
Seeks to maintain rigid appointment schedule	Reacts as the day's events evolve

A2: Low/High Context Chart

Low-Context Culture	High-Context Culture
Believes in explicit (literal) communication	Utilizes figurative and approximate language
Follows the letter of the law	Believes laws can be shaped by circumstances
Keeps job tasks separate from relationships	Sees task as a function of the relationship
Uses direct style in writing and speaking	Prefers indirect style in writing and speaking
Values individual initiative and decision making	Expects decision making within the relationship
Relies on verbal communication	Relies on nonverbal communication
Becomes uncomfortable with silence	Respects and utilizes silence
Presents facts, statistics, and other details	Subordinates use of detailed information

A3: Mechanistic/Humanistic View of Employee Chart

Mechanistic Employee	Humanistic Employee
Works for employer in exchange for wages and benefits	Thinks of self as group member with personal ties
Changes jobs if better opportunity arises	Remains on the job out of loyalty to "family"
Can be dismissed if not performing job satisfactorily	Keeps job even if performance is unsatisfactory
Views self as a commodity	Views self as part of a "family"

AUDIENCE ANALYSIS WORKSHEET

Who is my primary audience (actual receiver of my oral or written message)?

_____

What do I know about him/her/them personally and professionally (age, gender, education, job responsibility and status, civic and religious affiliation, knowledge of subject, cultural background)?_____

_____

_____

What is his/her/their attitude about me? _____

About my subject? _____

About being there to receive my message?_____

What does my audience *want* to know about my subject?_____

_____

What do I *need* my audience to know? _____

_____

What is the *consistent concern* that I always hear from my audience? _____

_____

What specific information addresses that concern?_____

_____

Who is my hidden/secondary audience?_____

What do I know about him/her/them? _____

_____

What is the *consistent concern* of my hidden/secondary audience?

_____

What specific information addresses that concern?_____

_____

Who is the decision maker? _____

What do I know about him/her?_____

_____

What is the *consistent concern* of the decision maker? _____

_____

What specific information addresses that concern?_____

_____

Other observations: _____

_____

_____

EXAMPLE B1 — AUDIENCE ANALYSIS WORKSHEET FOR MACY*S PRESENTATION

SPEAKER: Mark Sakowski, Operations Manager

Who is my primary audience (actual receiver of my oral or written information)?
*Newly hired Macy*s sales associates.*

What do I know about them personally and professionally (age, gender, education, job responsibility and status, civic and religious affiliation, knowledge of subject, cultural background)?
Diverse backgrounds. Limited knowledge of subject. Diversity in all other categories.

What is their attitude about me?
Open. They expect I have some power, but they are unsure.

About my subject?
Open. They want to learn all aspects of customer service and satisfaction.

About being there to receive my message?
Open. This is all new to them.

What does my audience *want* to know about my subject?
What they will get out of it.

What do I *need* my audience to know?
How they can financially benefit from offering instant credit to our customers, today and in the future.

What is the *consistent concern* that I always hear from my audience?
What's in it for me?

What specific information addresses that concern?
How they can financially benefit today, in the near future, and in the long term by opening charge accounts for customers.

Who is my hidden/secondary audience?

The company training director.

What do I know about her?

She hired the trainer who heard an earlier presentation and gave me feedback. As a result, she has specific expectations of the quality of my material and the details of my PowerPoint presentation. She expects me to improve my opening and benefits.

What is the *consistent concern* of my hidden/secondary audience?

To see obvious improvement from training.

What specific information addresses that concern?

I am doing everything the trainer asked me to do.

Who is the decision maker?

N/A for this presentation, except maybe also training director.

AUDIENCE ANALYSIS WORKSHEET FOR BENETTON PRESENTATION

SPEAKER: Sean Mayberry, a consultant hired by the Industrial Policy Committee of Italy to advise them on various courses of action to prevent the Benetton Company from moving out of Italy. (This presentation was prepared for an MBA International Perspectives course.)

Who is my primary audience (actual receiver of my oral or written message)?

Industrial Policy Committee of Italy.

What do I know about them personally and professionally (age, gender, education, job responsibility and status, civic and religious affiliation, knowledge of subject, cultural background)?

Older; all professionals; appointed to their positions on the Committee; held accountable for actions by elected officials and, ultimately, the voters.

What is their attitude about me?

Curious; open-minded.

About my subject?

Serious; hopeful about my recommendations.

About being there to receive my message?

Anxious, because they need assistance.

What does my audience *want* to know about my subject?

How my recommendations will help correct their current problems.

What do I *need* my audience to know?

That my recommendations are correct.

What is the *consistent concern* that I always hear from my audience?

How much they need guidance in formulating an Italian industrial policy that encourages firms such as Benetton to remain in Italy despite the high costs associated with being located in that country.

What specific information addresses that concern?

1. *Tax incentives/credits will reduce the cost of building and operating a factory in Italy.*

2. *Managed trade (i.e., tariffs on imported apparel products) decreases competition against Italian firms and permits these firms to become "lazy" and hence less able to compete in the global marketplace.*

Who is my hidden/secondary audience?

Executives of the Benetton Company itself.

What do I know about them?

Little personal information.

What is the consistent concern of my hidden/secondary audience?

That the current situation in Italy may force Benetton's relocation to less costly countries, and that Benetton may lose the numerous advantages it enjoys while being located in Italy (e.g., skilled apparel labor, highly developed fashion industry).

What specific information addresses that concern?

Same as above.

Who is the decision maker?

The chairman of the Industrial Policy Committee.

What do I know about him?

Very little, except that he is looking for outside opinions and guidance.

What is the consistent concern of the decision maker?

To do what is best for Italy.

What specific information addresses that concern?

Same as above.

Other observations:

None.

INTRODUCTION

- **Attention-getter.** Based on what I know about my primary audience, what will get his/her/their attention (and also relate to topic and situation)?

  _____

- **Purpose.** As a result of this message, what do I want my audience *to do*?

  _____

- Are there any reasons I should be *indirect* with the purpose of this message (including cultural considerations)? If so, how should I temper my expressed goals?

  _____

- **Road map.** How am I going to accomplish my objectives; that is, what is my *agenda* for delivering the message?

  _____

- **Benefit for audience.** What's in it for them, *specifically and personally*?

  _____

CONCLUSION

- **Summary.** Exactly what do I want my audience *to remember* (the essence of my main points)?

  _____

  _____

- **Specific action.** Exactly what do I want my audience *to do*?

  _____

- **Strong final statement.** What is the *last thought* I want to leave with them?

  _____

BODY

Choose from these common options:

1. Chronological order for simple, ordered instructions or reports
2. Problem (3 parts) and solution (1 part) for audience with low knowledge
3. Problem (1 part) and solution (3 parts) for audience with high knowledge (Note: Your solution should include potential risks.)
4. Current situation and proposed situation (3/1 or 1/3, based on audience knowledge)
5. Inductive (general to specific) or deductive (specific to general)
6. Pros and cons (or compare and contrast) for simple analyses or evaluations
7. Decision making or problem solving for complex issues (Example D2)
8. Bad news format for information they do not want to hear (Example D3)

- **Point One:**_____

  Support Material (such as statistics or examples): _____

  _____

  _____

  _____

- **Point Two:**_____

  Support Material: _____

  _____

  _____

  _____

- **Point Three:** _____

  Support Material: _____

  _____

  _____

  _____

- **Point Four:** _____

  Support Material: _____

  _____

  _____

  _____

OUTLINE WORKSHEET FOR MACY*S PRESENTATION

SPEAKER: Mark Sakowski, Operations Manager

AUDIENCE: Newly hired Macy*s Sales Associates. (Please see Example B1, Audience Analysis Worksheet for Macy*s Presentation.)

INTRODUCTION

- **Attention-getter.** Based on what I know about my primary audience, what will get their attention?

  Ability to make additional money!

- **Purpose.** As a result of this presentation, what do I want the audience *to do*?

  *Open Macy*s charge accounts for customers.*

- (Are there any reasons I should be *indirect* with the purpose of this message?)

  No.

- **Road map.** How am I going to accomplish my objectives; that is, what is my *agenda* for delivering the message?

  *Give specific examples of how opening Macy*s charge accounts will lead to making more money.*

- **Benefit for audience.** What's in it for them, *specifically and personally*?

  Financial gain.

CONCLUSION

- **Summary.** Exactly what do I want my audience *to remember*?

  *Opening a Macy*s charge account for a customer will pay off for them today and for a long time to come.*

- **Specific action.**   Exactly what do I want my audience *to do?*
    *Open Macy*s charge accounts for customers.*

- **Strong final statement.**   What is the *last thought* I want to leave with them?
    Cash in now!

BODY

Choose:

1. Chronological order for simple, ordered instructions
2. Problem (3 parts) and solution (1 part) for audience with low knowledge
3. Problem (1 part) and solution (3 parts) for audience with high knowledge
4. Situation current and situation proposed (3/1 or 1/3, based on audience knowledge)
5. Inductive (general to specific) or deductive (specific to general)
6. Decision making or problem solving for complex issues
7. Pro and con for simple comparisons
8. Bad news for information they do not want to hear

- **Point One:**
    Associates can earn a minimum of $3 with each account they open.

    Support Material:
    It adds up into money for trips, cars, etc.

- **Point Two:**
    The additional card holders will help them get a better raise.

    Support Material:
    Associates will lower selling costs; card holders spend more money.

- **Point Three:**
    Long-term client sales will lead to future raises.

    Support Material:
    It is easy to make credit applicants into long-term clients.

OUTLINE WORKSHEET FOR BENETTON PRESENTATION

SPEAKER: Sean Mayberry, a consultant hired by the Industrial Policy Committee of Italy to advise them on various courses of action to prevent the Benetton Company from moving out of Italy. (This presentation was prepared for an MBA International Perspectives course.)

AUDIENCE: Industrial Policy Committee of Italy. (Please see Example B2, Audience Analysis Worksheet for Benetton Presentation.)

INTRODUCTION

- **Attention-getter.** Based on what I know about my primary audience, what will get their attention?

  Possible loss of tax revenues and local employment from Benetton.

- **Purpose.** As a result of this presentation, what do I want the audience *to do*?

  Accept and implement both of my recommendations.

- (Are there any reasons I should be *indirect* with the purpose of this message?)

  Absolutely not. However, I will remember to address my audience respectfully.

- **Road map.** How am I going to accomplish my objectives; that is, what is my *agenda* for delivering the message?

  Background.
  Directions.
  Threats (problem).
  Options, recommendations (solutions).

- **Benefit for audience.** What's in it for them, *specifically and personally*?

  Opportunity to correct deficiencies in Italian industrial policy. Enhance probability of re-election for the officials who appointed these members of the Industrial Policy Committee (and hence increase the likelihood that these members themselves will remain on the committee).

CONCLUSION

- **Summary.**   Exactly what do I want my audience *to remember* (essence of main points)?

  Italy derives numerous benefits from the presence of Benetton in that country. However, because of the future plans Benetton is undertaking, it is increasingly likely that Benetton will begin to move more of its presence from Italy to lower-cost nations (such as China). Therefore, in order to reduce the cost that Benetton is faced with while operating in Italy and hence compete with these lower-cost nations, I recommend the following for Italy:

  1. *Implement tax incentives/credits that reduce the costs to Benetton of building and operating additional production plants in Italy, which are necessary as Benetton increases worldwide sales.*

  2. *Reject managed trade By allowing non-Italian firms to compete with Italian apparel firms on a level playing field, the Italian firms will be forced to lower their costs if they intend to remain in business. Benetton will benefit by lowering its own costs and also by contracting its business with now less costly Italian firms.*

- **Specific action.**   Exactly what do I want my audience *to do?*

  Accept both recommendations.

- **Strong final statement.**   What is the *last thought* I want to leave with them?

  Benetton's movement out of Italy is a very real possibility that will negatively affect the Italian national economy. Strong action is required by the Industrial Policy Committee in order to avoid this action by Benetton. Surely you do not want the next Benetton labels to read "Made in China."

BODY

Choose from these common options:

1. Chronological order for simple, ordered instructions
2. Problem (3 parts) and solution (1 part) for audience with low knowledge (Note: The speaker chose to present 5 main points: background, 3 parts of the problem, and the solution.)

3. Problem (1 part) and solution (3 parts) for audience with high knowledge
4. Current situation and proposed situation (3/1 or 1/3, based on audience knowledge)
5. Inductive (general to specific) or deductive (specific to general)
6. Pros and cons (or compare and contrast) for simple analyses or evaluations
7. Decision making or problem solving for complex issues (Appendix D)
8. Bad news for information they do not want to hear (Appendix D)

- **Point One:** *Benetton background.*
  Support Material (such as statistics or examples):
  > *Formed in the 1960s.*
  > *Sales of $2.5 billion in 1995.*
  > *Worldwide presence.*

- **Point Two:** *Importance of Benetton to Italy.*
  Support Material:
  > *Employs 4,300 Italian workers.*
  > *Pays $140 million in taxes to Italy.*
  > *Contracts out business to 900 Italian apparel firms.*

- **Point Three:** *Benetton future plans.*
  Support Material:
  > *Increase its global presence.*
  > *Focus on expansion in the Middle East and China.*
  > *Contracts out business to 900 Italian apparel firms.*
  > *Lower costs.*
  > *Move production out of Italy.*

- **Point Four:** *High costs in Italy.*
  Support Material:
  > *Very expensive labor.*
  > *High costs of capital (Italian factory costs three to five times more than Chinese factory).*

- **Point Five:** *Two recommendations to reverse current trends.*
  Support Material:
  > *Implement tax incentives/credits.*
  > *Reject managed trade.*

APPENDIX D

BASIC ORGANIZATIONAL PLANS

The following three basic, flexible outline models provide organizational plans that may apply to any communication situation you may encounter.

The Basic Outline Model (Appendix D1) is the most universal. Note the opportunities for variety in the body of the outline. See Examples D1.1 and D1.2.

The Problem-Solving Model (Appendix D2) works best for complex presentations, reports, or meeting agendas that require careful justification of your reasoning. Pay particular attention to the step that requires you to articulate criteria for a successful solution *before* you begin brainstorming. See Examples D2.1 and D2.2.

Keep these points in mind when using the **Basic Outline Model** and the **Problem-Solving Model**:

- The information in the **Introduction** does not have to be in order, but you must include information that focuses your audience's attention, states your purpose, specifies your agenda (road map), and establishes benefit for your audience.

- The information in the **Conclusion** must summarize the essence of your main points and ask for a specific action. Your final comment may be a part of your action step or a separate sentence; your last statement may *not* be part of your summary.

The Bad News Model (Appendix D3) is appropriate any time you are communicating information that your audience will not want to hear. Always offer reasons that your receivers want to know and alternatives that will soften the effects of the bad news. Note that the Body of the Bad News Model can stand alone without Introduction and Conclusion. See Examples D3.1 and D3.2.

BASIC OUTLINE MODEL

INTRODUCTION

- **Attention-getter.** Based on your analysis of your audience, what will get their attention?
- **Purpose.** As a result of this message, what exactly do you want your audience *to do*?
- **Road map (agenda).** What steps will you go through in this message in order to meet your goals?
- **Benefit for audience.** What is in this for them, *specifically and personally*?

BODY

(Choose from these common options. Remember to *limit* main points.)

1. Chronological order for simple, ordered instructions or reports
2. Problem (3 parts) and solution (1 part) for audience with low knowledge
3. Problem (1 part) and solution (3 parts) for audience with high knowledge (Note: Your solution should include potential risks.)
4. Current situation and proposed situation (3/1 or 1/3, based on audience knowledge)
5. Inductive (general to specific) or deductive (specific to general)
6. Pros and cons (or compare and contrast) for simple analyses or evaluations
7. Decision making or problem solving for complex issues
8. Bad news format for information they do not want to hear

CONCLUSION

(You may ask for questions here.)

- **Summary.** What do you want your audience *to remember* (the essence of your main points)?
    (You may ask for questions here.)
- **Action step.** What do you want your audience *to do* (specific action)?
    (You may ask for questions here.)
- **Final statement.** What is the *last thought* you want to leave with your audience?
    (No questions here!)

EXAMPLE
D1.1

OUTLINE FOR MACY*S PRESENTATION

SPEAKER: Mark Sakowski, Operations Manager

AUDIENCE: Newly hired Macy*s Sales Associates. (Please see Example B1, Audience Analysis Worksheet for Macy*s Presentation, and Example C1, Outline Worksheet for Macy*s Presentation.)

INTRODUCTION

- Attention-getter.

   *"May I put this on your Macy*s card?" is the phrase that pays in CASH for you!*

- Purpose, road map, and benefit for receiver.

   *"May I put this on your Macy*s card?"*

   > *Pays you...CASH today!*
   > *Pays you...CASH in the near future!*
   > *Pays you...CASH for years to come!*

BODY

- CASH today.

   > *$3.00 for every application.*
   > *Special credit promotions.*
   > *CASH you can use today.*
   > *Or, save it for a trip, down payment...*
   > *IT'S UP TO YOU!*

- CASH in the near future.

   > *Credit customers spend more.*

Increase your personal sales.
Lower your selling cost.
Larger raise.

- CASH for years to come.
  Credit applications.
    Excellent client information.
    For years to come...
    Increased sales.
    Larger raises.

CONCLUSION

- Summary.
  Remember:
  *"May I put this on your Macy*s card?"*
    Pays you...CASH today!
    Pays you...CASH in the near future!
    Pays you...CASH for years to come!

- Action step and final statement.
  It's the phrase that pays...so cash in NOW!

OUTLINE FOR BENETTON PRESENTATION

SPEAKER: Sean Mayberry, a consultant hired by the Industrial Policy Committee of Italy to advise them on various courses of action to prevent the Benetton Company from moving out of Italy. (This presentation was prepared for an MBA International Perspectives course.)

AUDIENCE: Italy's Industrial Policy Committee. (Please see Example B2, Audience Analysis Worksheet for Benetton Presentation, and Example C2, Outline Worksheet for Benetton Presentation.)

INTRODUCTION

- **Attention-getter.**
  - a. *Benneton's use of "shocking" material for its ads compared to the conventional approaches used by other firms.*
  - b. *You could lose tax revenues and local employment from Benetton.*

- **Purpose.**
  - *To convince the Committee to alter its policy and hence provide a positive economic environment for the Benetton Company in Italy.*

- **Road map.**
  - a. *Provide background on Benetton.*
  - b. *Explain Benetton's economic importance to Italy.*
  - c. *Explain Benetton's future directions.*
  - d. *Provide examples of high operating costs in Italy.*
  - e. *Explain how Benetton's new directions are a threat to the government of Italy.*
  - f. *Provide recommendations that Italy may take in order to keep Benetton in Italy.*

- **Benefit for audience.**
  - a. *Maintain significant tax flows from Benetton.*
  - b. *Maintain sizable employment for Italian workers.*

      c. Enhance probability of re-election for government officials who appoint the members of the Industrial Policy Committee.

BODY

- **Provide background on Benetton.**
- **Explain Benetton's importance to Italy.**
- **Explain Benetton's new directions.**
- **Provide examples of high operating costs in Italy.**
- **Explain the negative impact that Benetton's relocation from Italy will have on Italy.**
- **Provide recommendations that Italy may take in order to keep Benetton in Italy.**

CONCLUSION

- **Summary.**

  Remember:

  a. The current industrial environment in Italy is NOT supporting Benetton.

  b. Action is required on the part of the government to correct this situation.

- **Action step ("do").**

  Accept these recommendations:

  a. Implement tax incentives/credits that will reduce the costs that Benetton experiences in Italy.

  b. Reject managed trade; allow foreign firms to compete with Italian firms. This will ultimately "force" the Italian firms to innovate, become more efficient, and lower their costs.

- **Final statement.**

  Do you want the Benetton label to read "Made in China"?

APPENDIX

D2 PROBLEM-SOLVING MODEL

INTRODUCTION

- **Attention-getter.** Based on what you know about your audience, what will get their attention?
- **Purpose.** As a result of this messge, exactly what do you want your audience *to do?*
- **Road map (agenda).** What steps will you go through in this message in order to meet your goals?
- **Benefit for audience.** What is in this for them, *specifically and personally?*

BODY

- **Define** the issue or **problem**.
- **Establish** a checklist of **criteria** for a successful solution.
- **List** (relevant, feasible, limited) possible **solutions**.
- **Evaluate solutions** based on the established criteria.
- **Select** the **best solution**.
- **Discuss implementation.** Employ dimensions of the **CrossTalk** Communication Model that may apply:

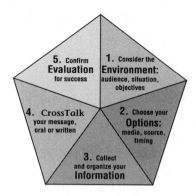

CONCLUSION

- **Summary.** What do you want your audience to remember (the essence of your main points)?
- **Action Step.** What do you want your audience *to do?*
- **Final Statement.** What is the *last thought* you want to leave with them?

PROBLEM-SOLVING OUTLINE FOR ATLANTA GAS LIGHT PRESENTATION

SPEAKER: James A. Cika, Laboratory Engineer, Atlanta Gas Light Company (AGLC)

AUDIENCE: Management personnel, including two vice presidents, responsible for maintaining the facilities of AGLC. Meeting has been called to discuss temperature control problems in the Materials Management and Testing Facility, including the R&D Laboratory. Few present will know either me or my prior job experience.

INTRODUCTION

- **Attention-getter.**

  Frightening questions about the safety of the lab.

- **Statement of purpose.**

  To persuade you to start the process of installing a new heating, ventilation, and air-conditioning (HVAC) system in the lab.

- **Road map.**

  Discuss current unsafe situation.

  Explain criteria for solution.

  Identify options.

  Explain best option.

  Discuss implementation.

- **Benefit for listeners.**

  Cleaner environment in lab and other areas of the building.

  More accurate reports for your needs.

  Quicker advancement in natural gas air-conditioning technology, on which the company, and therefore our jobs, depend.

BODY

- **Define the problem.**

  Current HVAC design is not adequate for a laboratory test facility.

- **Criteria for solution.**

  Lab temperature and humidity.
  Isolated environment with adequate exhaust.
  Secured controls.

- **Options.**

  Redesign current HVAC system.
  Design and install new HVAC system.
  Construct new lab facility and relocate lab.

- **Best option.**

  Current system cannot be redesigned, based on past performance.
  New lab facility would be too expensive and take too long to build.
  Therefore, design and install new system.

QUESTIONS

CONCLUSION

- **What to remember.**

  A safe lab and Materials Management Testing Facility depends on a proper HVAC system.
  The credibility of lab reports for your needs depends on a proper HVAC system.

- **What to do.**

  Begin process to design and install a new HVAC system in the lab immediately.
  Final statement.
  Although costs may be high, the reputation of the company and the health of some of its employees depend on the installation of a new HVAC system.

EXAMPLE D2.2

PROBLEM-SOLVING OUTLINE FOR TADELLE CHOCOLATE BARS PRESENTATION

BACKGROUND: *Tadelle* is a brand name chocolate bar that the Sagra Company of Turkey has been producing since 1957. For decades, it was the market leader, both for its great taste and its reasonable price. However, sales began to decline gradually over the past years, and *Tadelle* lost a great portion of its market share. Most consumers of *Tadelle* are over thirty years old.

SPEAKER: Tolga Yaveroglu, Marketing Department

AUDIENCE: The top management team of Sagra Company, meeting to discuss the low sales of their number-one brand *Tadelle*. They have invited the marketing department to identify the reason for the problem and to offer solutions.

INTRODUCTION

- **Attention step.**
    Disturbing facts about the sales of Tadelle.

- **Statement of purpose.**
    Create a new image for Tadelle.

- **Benefit for audience.**
    Increase in market share.
    New consumers purchasing Tadelle.
    Double-digit growth in sales and revenues.

BODY

- **Define the nature of the problem.**
    Current image is old-fashioned.
    People want change.
    New products are gaining prominence.

- **Determine the criteria for the best solution.**
  Something new; not old-fashioned.
  New customers.
  Low costs during process.
  Quick answer.

- **Identify possible solutions.**
  A totally new product.
  A new image for Tadelle.

- **Select best solution, based on criteria.**
  A totally new product: risky, costly, time-consuming.
  Therefore: a new image for Tadelle.

- **Implement solution.**
  New package color.
  New ad: Young lovers.
  New motto: "The best way of expressing feelings."

CONCLUSION

- **What to remember.**
  Creating new images means creating new profits.

- **What to do.**
  Create new image.
  Start campaigns.

- **Strong final statement.**
  We can only survive this way.

D3 BAD NEWS MODEL

INTRODUCTION

- **Attention-getter.** Based on your analysis of your audience, what will get their attention?
- **Purpose.** As a result of this message, what exactly do you what your audience *to do*?
- **Road map (agenda).** What steps will you go through in this message in order to meet your goals?
- **Benefit for audience.** What is in this for them, specifically and personally?

BODY

(Note: A bad news *letter* may include only the following six points, thus standing alone without Introduction and Conclusion)

- **Cushion** your audience. Select information that establishes goodwill but does not contradict your bad news message.
- Bridge with a **transition**. You may say simply "however," or use a sentence.
- Deliver the **bad news**. Be specific.
- Explain the **reasons** for the bad news. Avoid nebulous or ambiguous reasons, such as, "It's company policy." (Note: You may explain your reason *first*, before you give the bad news.)
- Suggest **alternatives**. Offer the receiver of the bad news some other options.
- Rebuild **goodwill**. Return the focus of your message to something positive that you share with your audience.

CONCLUSION

(You may ask for questions here.)

- **Summary.** What do you want your audience *to remember* (the essence of your main points)?
  (You may ask for questions here.)
- **Action step.** What do you want your audience *to do* (specific action)?
  (You may ask for questions here.)
- **Final statement.** What is the *last thought* you want to leave with your audience?
  (No questions here!)

EXAMPLE

D3.1

BAD NEWS LETTER

The Journal

Scott Peterson, Jr., Ph.D., Editor
Department of Management Communication
College of Business, Chicago University
Chicago, Illinois 23444-3444

July 13, 1996

Professor John Howard
Decision Sciences Department
Centenary College
Shreveport, Louisiana 70634-1314

Dear Professor Howard:

(**Cushion reader.**) Thank you for submitting your manuscript, "Attitudes to Behavior," to *The Journal*. We appreciate the opportunity to examine your research.

(**Transition.**) However, (**Reasons.**) our review board has raised several concerns about your paper. I have enclosed their detailed comments for your review. (**Bad news.**) As a result, I believe that "Attitudes to Behavior" is not appropriate for *The Journal* at this time.

(**Alternatives.**) If you choose to revise your manuscript, I would be pleased to ask the same reviewers to give it another look. You might also consider submitting it to *The Bulletin*, which, as you know, publishes applied communication papers.

(**Rebuild goodwill.**) Thank you again for submitting your paper. I wish you the best of luck with your research.

Sincerely,

Scott Peterson, Jr.

Scott Peterson, Jr., Ph.D.
Editor

Enclosures

SMH TECHNOLOGIES, INC.

11480 Northwest Industrial Drive * Santa Rosana, California * (234) 234-2222

March 29, 1996

Mr. James Womeldorf, President
Photo Research Dynamics
1111 Broad Street
Mason, IL 54321-1111

Dear Mr. Womeldorf:

(Cushion reader.) As you may already know, recent developments within our industry have forced my organization to realign its efforts along certain high volume product lines.

(Transition.) Unfortunately, as a result, we are having to reassess some of our supplier relationships. **(Bad news.)** As an integral part of our re-alignment strategy, we have decided to discontinue producing the KX-11 surveillance satellite.

(Reasons.) As you know, the end of the cold war and a desire on Capitol Hill to reduce the budget deficit have combined to reduce defense-oriented spending. These budget cuts have greatly affected our firm, and we are currently shifting our efforts toward more commercially viable products and technologies. Unfortunately, your firm's SLK 2300 infrared camera is unsuitable for commercial use.

(Alternative.) However, we currently are designing a new weather satellite that may utilize this type of technology. If your firm should chose to focus its efforts on alternative applications for this technology, we would certainly be willing to discuss future projects.

(Rebuild goodwill.) SMH Technologies has enjoyed the working relationship that we have had with your firm for the past 20 years. In addition, we look forward to any future opportunities to continue our relationship.

Sincerely,

Samuel M. Hawkins

Samuel M. Hawkins
Chairman and CEO

SMH: dav

APPENDIX E

ADDITIONAL SAMPLE PRESENTATION OUTLINES

The following three outlines further exemplify applications of the outline models.

EXAMPLE E1

PROBLEM-SOLVING PRESENTATION OUTLINE FOR SEXUAL HARASSMENT

SPEAKER: Liliana Roman, Human Resources Manager

AUDIENCE: Monthly Management Meeting, Avatar Company

INTRODUCTION

- **Attention-getter.**
  Extreme example of potential damage that sexual harassment can cause for a firm.

- **Purpose.**
  Educate managers on how to stop harassment.

- **Benefit for receivers.**
  Preserve future of the firm and also your careers.

BODY

- *Costs associated with sexual harassment* (problem).
  Legal fees and penalties.
  Internal discord.
  Professional and corporate reputations.

- *Program to prevent incurring costs* (solution).
  Establish clear guidelines.
  Train managers.
  Educate staff.
  Establish support committee.

CONCLUSION

- **What to remember.**
  Preventing sexual harassment will preserve our firm.

- **What to do.**
  Implement a plan to reduce liability and increase credibility and reputation.

- **Final statement.**
  Costs of the problem far outweigh the costs of prevention.

EXAMPLE
E2

COMPARE AND CONTRAST PRESENTATION OUTLINE PRICE COMPARISONS: UNITED STATES AND JAPAN

SPEAKER: Satoshi Abe, Manager, International Manufacturing Firm

AUDIENCE: Colleagues who are going to Japan for the first time

INTRODUCTION

- **Attention-getter.**
  Japan's population and land size, as compared to that of the United States.

- **Purpose.**
  To introduce you to some differences between the United States and Japan.

- **Road map.**
  Examples of simple comparisons.

- **Benefit for audience.**
  To recognize similarities in differences and thus be more comfortable in Japan.

BODY

- *Apartment rent with examples.*
- *Food prices with examples.*
- *Fuel prices with examples.*
- *Travel costs with examples.*

CONCLUSION

- **What to remember.**

  Though there are many differences between our two countries, there are good points and bad points in both.

- **What to do.**

  Be aware of the differences and enjoy them.

- **Last thought.**

  I wish you very good luck in Japan.

PROBLEM-SOLVING PRESENTATION OUTLINE FOR HAUSSER FOOD PRODUCTS

BACKGROUND: Hausser Food Products is a leading manufacturer of baby food in the US. In response to a flat sales, Housser hired consultant Morgan Mitra to study methods of boosting sales. As a result of his research in the Southeastern region, Mitra discovered that baby food was popular with the senior citizens of Florida. However, the Florida sales team was hiding this market segment so they could meet their annually increasing sales quota without expending much extra effort. Since the company was not aware of the senior citizen market potential, they had missed the opportunity to market to this segment nationwide.

SPEAKER: Morgan Mitra, Marketing Consultant

AUDIENCE: Executive Management Team, Hausser Food Products

INTRODUCTION

- **Attention-getter.**

  Hausser Food Products has implemented a flawed incentive pay plan that reduces productivity. The result is a built-in incentive to work against management.

- **Purpose.**

  Implement a three-step plan to overhaul the incentive compensation system.

- **Road map.**

  Problems with the current plan.
  Sources of the problems.
  Solution.

- **Audience benefit.**

  Motivated workforce that is more productive.
  Increased corporate sales and profitability.

BODY

- *Problems associated with current incentive pay plan.*
    Unmotivated workforce.
    "Us vs. them" attitude toward management.

- *Sources of problems.*
    Invisible decisions.
    Sales targets revised upward annually.

- *Solution.*
    Open the books of the company to the workers.
    Allow employee input in determining sales targets.
    Restructure incentive pay plan: Link bonuses to company profitability.

CONCLUSION

- **Restatement of purpose.**
    I recommend this three-step plan to overhaul the incentive compensation system.

- **Summary.**
    Problems:
        Unmotivated workforce.
        "Us vs. them" attitude.
        Invisible decisions.
        Adjusted sales targets.
    Solutions:
        Open the books.
        Involve employees.
        Restructure incentive pay plan.

- **Strong final statement.**
    The Florida sales team met yearly sales goals by deceiving management and working against the company. This new incentive plan will help you meet your goals with salespersons and management working together to achieve a better financial future.

APPENDIX

F

GUIDELINES FOR VISUAL AIDS

- **Select the appropriate type of visual aids.** To decide, first refer to your analysis of your audience, situation, objective, and corporate culture. Then evaluate the actual venue in which you will be speaking. As a basic rule, the bigger the group, the larger and more formal your visual aids. Here are your options with some of the advantages and disadvantages of each.

PRESENTATION VISUAL AID OPTIONS WITH ADVANTAGES AND DISADVANTAGES OF EACH

OPTION	ADVANTAGES	DISADVANTAGES
Models, objects	Offer realism Provide hands-on experience Are appropriate for all cultures	Cannot be seen by large groups Detract from speaker
Write-on boards, flip charts, write-on transparencies	May be generated by audience Create casual atmosphere Appear spontaneous	Indicate lack of preparation Take time during presentation Require good handwriting Are not appropriate for formal cultures
Prepared flipcharts	Transport anywhere	Cannot be seen by large groups Are not appropriate for formal cultures
Handouts	Add note-taking capabilities Are appropriate for all cultures	Distract from speaker

Our choice for most presentations:

Computer-generated overhead transparencies (commonly called *slides*)	Appear professional Indicate preparation Work in lighted room Require only overhead projector Are appropriate for all cultures	Require backup bulbs
Photographic slides	Show vibrant colors	Require darkened room Preclude returning to earlier point
Videocassettes	Show movement Provide variety	Require videocassette player and monitor large enough for audience to see Are expensive to produce
Computer-generated slides presented via computer	Appear professional	May require semi-darkened room Require Liquid Crystal Display (LCD) panel, computer, and overhead projector Cause embarrassing or annoying delays when technical difficulties arise
Multimedia productions	Create high-tech atmosphere Appear most impressive of all options	Require complex, advanced computer hardware and software for preparation and presentation Distract from speaker Could overwhelm or intimidate less sophisticated audiences or cultures

Remember, *you* are the most important visual element of your presentation, so your audience must be able to see you. Therefore, avoid any option that requires you to completely turn off the room lights.

 Although writing on transparencies and flip charts is acceptable for some business presentations in the United States, foreign audiences may perceive this spontaneity as a lack of preparation. As a rule, you should be more organized and formal with *any* international audience than you would be at home.

- **Use your Outline Worksheet.**   After you have selected and organized your material, prepare your visual aids. Your slides function as your notes, which enables you to appear more spontaneous and natural in your delivery. (Note: We use the term *slide* to refer to computer-generated transparencies, which require only an overhead projector, and slides presented from your computer via LCD panel and projector. The concepts, however, also apply to visual aids prepared for other media.)

- **Prepare one slide for each idea.**   For example, a basic presentation might have the following slides:

  1. Title
  2. Attention-getter
  3. Purpose
  4. Agenda (road map)
  5. Benefit for audience
  6. Point #1
  7. Support or example for point #1
  8. Point #2
  9. Support or example for point #2
  10. Point #3
  11. Support or example for point #3
  12. Summary (may be repeat of agenda)
  13. Action step
  14. Conclusion

- **Limit your slides based on the desired length of your speech.**   Figure on an average of one slide per minute. (Therefore, the speech for the preceding example would be approximately fourteen minutes.)

- **Keep it simple.**   Try to limit your material to five lines of copy on each slide. Use no more than seven points for maximum retention.

- **Choose an appropriate font.**   There are two basic types: serif (the letters stand on small platforms) and sans serif. Serif is traditional and easier to read. Sans serif is more contemporary.

Examples of serif:	Examples of sans serif:
Americana	Eras
Fenice	Eurostile
Novarese	Optima

- **Capitalize sparingly.**   A mixture of uppercase and lowercase letters creates a more natural and easy-to-read visual. You may print your titles in all uppercase letters although you may find that this takes up too much space. Capitalize only proper nouns and the *first* letter of the first word in each bullet point of body copy.

- **Be consistent on all these points:**

  Background. Presentation software allows you to select a template for the entire presentation.

  Font. All titles should be the same size of the same font, and all body copy should be the same size of the same font. For computer-generated transparencies and slides, we suggest a *minimum* size of 28 point for body copy and 36 point for titles in most standard fonts. The titles and body copy may be a different font style. Title fonts should be easily recognized as larger.

  Illustrations. Graphs and clip art should be a similar size, but they do not have to be at the same location on each slide.

- **Illustrate your data with pictures and charts.**   Illustrations should give your audience the idea, not the detail. Save detailed data for handouts. Select the type of chart based on the relationship you want to show. Your options are shown on the following page.

- **Use color.**   High contrast between background and text provides excellent visibility in a lighted room. The current standard is a dark background (usually blue) with white or yellow text. You are not restricted to this combination, but remember that cool, dark colors (blue) appear to move away from the audience, and warm, light colors (yellow) appear to move toward the audience. You might try colors that complement your company logo or that symbolize your message. Finally, consider colors that might be particularly appropriate for the country or culture of your audience.

- **Leave some white (empty) space.**   Artistically design your slides for attractiveness and readability by skipping space between your title and bullet points and between each bullet. If any of your bullet points require more than one line, skip more space *between* the bullets than *within* each bullet. Arrange illustrations to enhance the message in your bullet points.

- **Simplify, simplify, simplify.**   After you have designed your visual aids, edit for clarity and succinctness. The less information on a slide, the better your audience will retain it.

- **Have some fun.**   Even the most serious presentations will benefit from appropriate humor. In most cases, humor will enhance your message and contribute to your audience's interest and understanding. Remember, however, to always consider the appropriateness of humor for your foreign audience.

  Remember:

  - Visual aids are the final step in your preparation.
  - Pictures are more persuasive than numbers and words.
  - Consistency itself is a powerful message.
  - Less is always more.

Examples of Charts and the Usage of Each

Type of chart	Example	Use

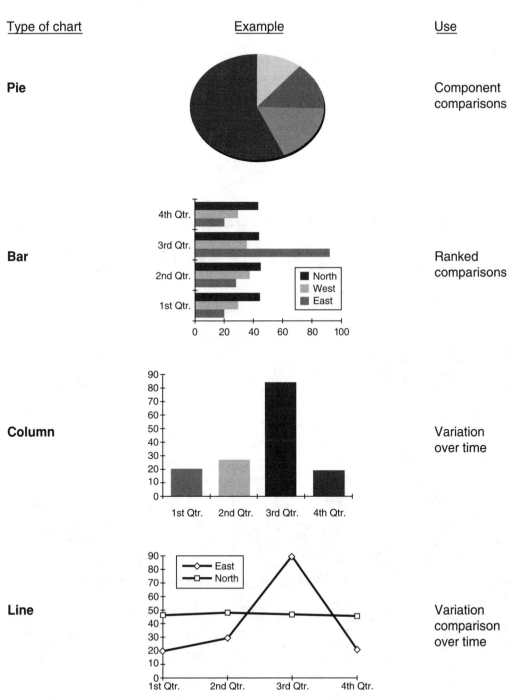

Pie — Component comparisons

Bar — Ranked comparisons

Column — Variation over time

Line — Variation comparison over time

In conclusion, consider this example from the O.J. Simpson trial. Prosecuting attorney Marcia Clark based her argument on the timeline illustrated in this visual aid.

Positive Aspects	*Negative Aspects*
Appropriate computer-generated transparency	Cluttered look from too much copy
Good use of uppercase and lowercase letters	Too many points for one visual
Consistent font	Words too small to read
Appropriate choice of high-contrast colors (blue background and yellow letters)	Not enough white space
	Certainly not simple!

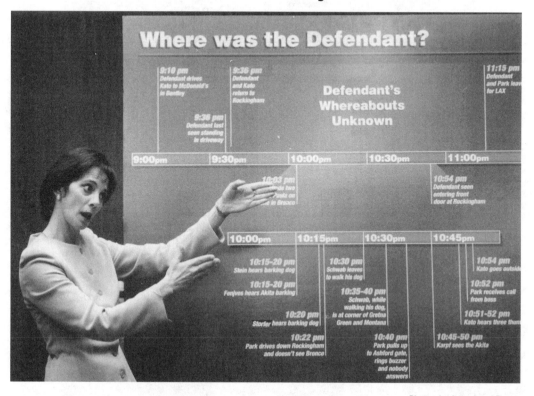

Photos by Associated Press.

Follow the truth to its logical conclusion, and you will convict O.J. Simpson, Marcia Clark tells jurors.

Suggested Readings

Boone, Louis E., and Kurtz, David L. *Contemporary Business Communication.* Englewood Cliffs, NJ: Prentice Hall, 1994.

Grauer, Robert T., and Barber, Maryann. *Exploring Microsoft PowerPoint.* Englewood Cliffs, NJ: Prentice Hall, 1994.

Guffy, Mary E. *Business Communication: Process and Product.* Belmont, CA: Wadsworth, 1994.

Lowe, Doug. *PowerPoint 4 for Windows for Dummies.* San Mateo, CA: IDG Books, 1994.

Munter, Mary. *Guide to Managerial Communication*, 3rd ed. Englewood Cliffs, NJ: Prentice Hall, 1992.

APPENDIX

G

SAMPLE VISUALS

The following three PowerPoint slide presentations exemplify the guidelines in Appendix F.

SAMPLE VISUAL AIDS
CrossTalk COMMUNICATION

SPEAKER: Sherron B. Kenton, Ph.D., Senior Partner in the consulting firm Strategic Corporate Communications.

AUDIENCE: Top performers of the Business Services Division, MCI Telecommunications Corporation, who were selected to participate in this Strategic Presentation Workshop.

This presentation illustrates the following points in Appendix F, Guidelines for Visual Aids:

- Slides follow the outline of the presentation (see inside cover) to therefore serve as notes for the presenter.
- Bullets are limited to six points per slide (five is better).
- Serif fonts are traditional and easy to read.
- Only the first letter of the first word in titles and bulleted points is capitalized.
- Background, font style and size, and clip art size are consistent.
- Clip art and one chart illustrate information.
- Dark blue background with yellow and white letters is traditional and effective.
- In the original color version, variegated blue background and red accents add artistic appeal. Space is skipped between bullets. Pictures enhance the message.
- Outline is simplified for slides.
- Speaker employs humorous clip art and entertaining design techniques.

The humor in these slides may diminish the perception of the importance of the message for some audiences in some cultures. Always carefully consider the information you compile on your Audience Analysis Worksheet (Appendix B) before you make your final decisions about embellishing your visual aids.

Example G1, Figure 1

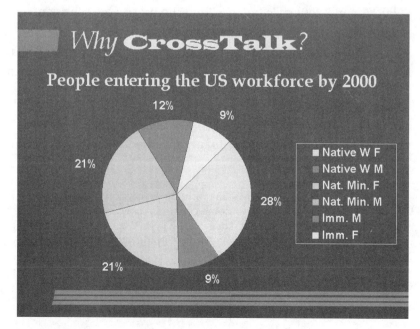

Example G1, Figure 2

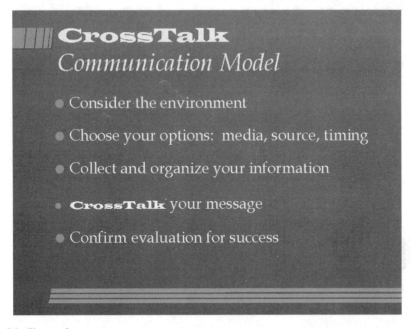

Example G1, Figure 3

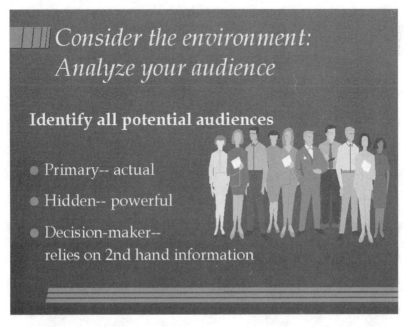

Example G1, Figure 4

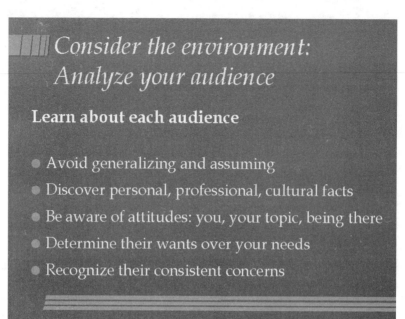

Example G1, Figure 5

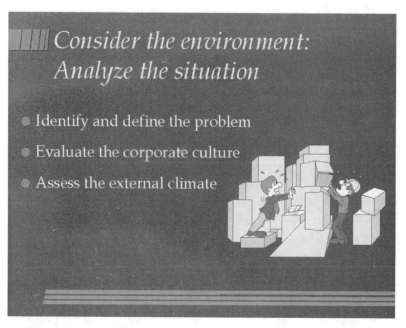

Example G1, Figure 6

Example G1, Figure 7

Example G1, Figure 8

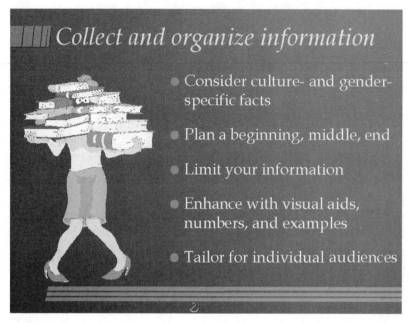

Example G1, Figure 9

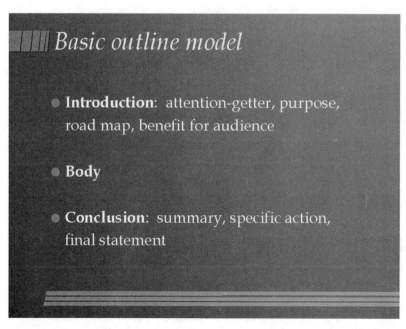

Example G1, Figure 10

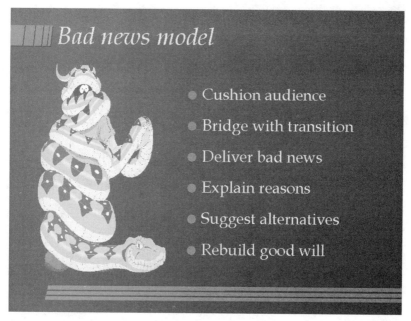

Example G1, Figure 11

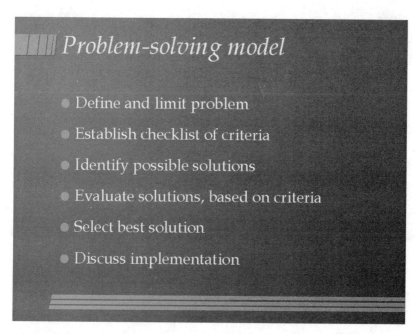

Example G1, Figure 12

Example G1, Figure 13

Example G1, Figure 14

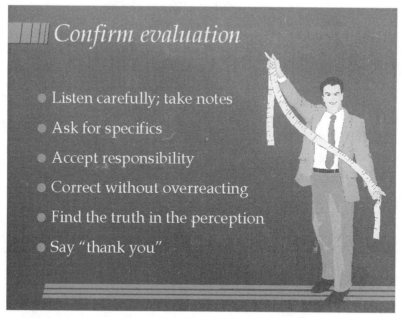

Example G1, Figure 15

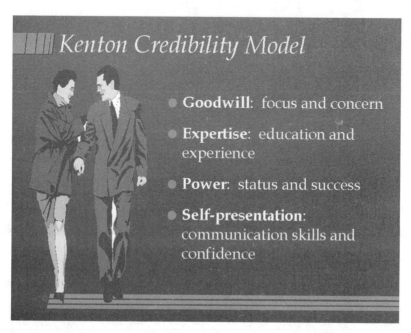

Example G1, Figure 16

Example G1, Figure 17

SAMPLE VISUAL AIDS
MACY*S PRESENTATION

SPEAKER: Mark Sakowski, Operations Manager

AUDIENCE: Newly hired Macy*s Sales Associates. (Please see Examples B1, Audience Analysis Worksheet; C1, Outline Worksheet; and D1.1, Outline for Macy*s Presentation.)

This presentation illustrates the following points in Appendix F, Guidelines for Visual Aids:

- Slides follow the outline of the presentation (see Example D1.1) to therefore serve as notes for the speaker.
- These seven slides are appropriate for a six-minute speech.
- The speaker limits his copy to five lines.
- Novarese, a serif font, is traditional and easy to read.
- The added capitalization enhances the message.
- Backgrounds, fonts, and illustrations are consistent.
- Clip art enhances the message. Note how the money piles up through points one, two, and three.
- In the original color version, the speaker used a dark green background to symbolize money.
- Artistic use of space enhances readability.
- These slides are simple and reinforcing.
- The speaker definitely employs humor.

The focus on money as motivation is most appropriate for an audience of young sales associates in the United States. If this presentation were delivered to a multi-cultural audience, the emphasis would focus on the consistent concerns of the particular audience revealed by the Audience Analysis Worksheet (Appendix B).

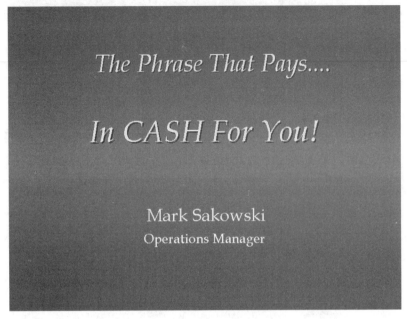

Example G2, Figure 1

Example G2, Figure 2

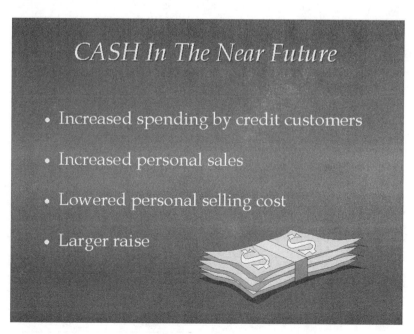

Example G2, Figure 3

Example G2, Figure 4

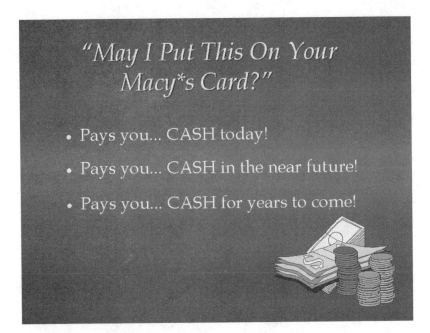

Example G2, Figure 5

Example G2, Figure 6

Example G2, Figure 7

SAMPLE VISUAL AIDS
BENETTON PRESENTATION

SPEAKER: Sean Mayberry, a consultant hired by the Industrial Policy Committee of Italy to advise them on various courses of action to take in order to prevent the Benetton Company from moving out of Italy. (This presentation was prepared for an MBA International Perspectives course.)

AUDIENCE: Italy's Industrial Policy Committee. (Please see Examples B2, Audience Analysis Worksheet; C2, Outline Worksheet; and D1.2, Outline for Benetton Presentation.)

This presentation illustrates the following points in Appendix F, Guidelines for Visual Aids:

- Slides follow the presentation outline, thus providing notes for the speaker.
- These eight slides are appropriate for a ten-minute presentation.
- The speaker minimizes his copy to five lines per slide.
- Optima is a contemporary sans serif font, indicating a modern, cutting-edge image.
- The speaker capitalizes appropriately.
- Background, font, and illustrations are consistent.
- Clip art enhances the message without distracting.
- In the original color version, dark blue, variegated background with yellow letters creates clean, easy-to-read visuals.
- Spacing enhances readability.
- Less is more.

Example G3, Figure 1

Example G3, Figure 2

Example G3, Figure 3

Example G3, Figure 4

Example G3, Figure 5

Example G3, Figure 6

Example G3, Figure 7

Example G3, Figure 8

APPENDIX H

PRESENTATION EVALUATION FORM

SPEAKER:

TOPIC:

SPEAKER'S TARGET AUDIENCE: EVALUATOR:

CONTENT:
* Relevant material for audience's knowledge level
* Acknowledgment of audience's wants and concerns
* Sufficient depth in support material, examples
* Follow-through to meet speaker's stated objectives

Strengths: **Needs Work:**

ORGANIZATION:
* Intro: attention, purpose, benefit, roadmap
* Body: limited points, clear plan
* Questions: controlled and succinct
* Conclusion: summary of main points, request for action, definite close

Strengths: **Needs Work:**

PRESENTATION:
* Vocal control and variety, including spontaneity and enthusiasm
* Physical control and variety, including eye contact, hand and body movement, facial expressions
* Preparation and handling of visual aids

Strengths: **Needs Work:**

Overall Comments:

Appendix I

Sample Letters, Memos, and Faxes

Although your writing will reflect your own culture, you will communicate more effectively if you are aware of the expectations of each of the other cultures. The more you know the individuals who represent your audience, the more effective your communication will become. Study the following writing information and samples for maximum effectiveness.

Example I1 Writing Samples of the Asian Audience

Typical Opening Statements for Japanese Letters

The letter usually contains three parts (opening, body, closing). The opening includes the seasonal greeting. These examples translated by Rumiko Mori are common.

(January)	It becomes much colder after the coldest day.
(February)	Plum blossoms bring spring.
(March)	Spring seems to come closer rain by rain.
(April)	Cherry blossoms come to bloom.
(May)	The air becomes warm, and the sky becomes blue.
(June)	The gloomy rainy season continues every day, and the Hydrangea gets wet from the rain.
(July)	The heat makes it unbearable.
(August)	Though the daytime is still hot, it becomes a little bit cooler in the morning and in the evening.
(September)	The chirps of insects become clearer, and the sounds of the chirps fill the sky.
(October)	Autumn becomes deeper, and the night becomes longer day by day.
(November)	Chilly winds soak into the body.
(December)	The days of this year become shorter. Here we have Christmas again.

Japanese Letter Example (Note: Letterheads are optional)

Address

Respectfully,

Though autumn becomes deeper and the night becomes longer day by day, I hope you work actively as usual.

Well, I moved to Atlanta this August to attend Emory University by my company's order. I want to take this opportunity to say thank you for your personal and professional association with me, when I worked at the network strategy department and the personnel department at Nippon Telephone and Telegraph.

Though I've not yet fully settled here and have had several concerns because this is my first experience to live abroad, I'm going to make a best effort to absorb as many things as possible during my limited stay in the U.S. I hope you will continue to give me the same support and helpful criticism as ever.

To close this letter, I would like to greet you with many thanks and hope for your health and further growth.

With great respect,
Rumiko Mori
1995. 10

Japanese Letter Example

Address

I write the following most respectfully,

The long lasting hot season is starting to fade away, and the chill in the mornings and evenings is showing the sign of approaching autumn. Be sure to take care of yourself at the turn of the seasons, as a change in the temperature is sometimes great these days.

Getting on to the main subject, I would like to thank you for the time you spent with me during my visit to Japan. The meetings I had with you were indeed enjoyable and rewarding.

It was particularly fascinating to hear how you analyzed the nature and extent of all the major causes of the problems we have been up against at US Trading for the past several years. You not only helped me clarify several important points which I had missed, but also pointed out some possible solutions to the problem. And, as a result, I now believe we should be able to come up with a workable solution sooner.

I would like to thank you again for all the help and valuable advice you have given me, and I hope that you will continue to favor us with your generous support. I look forward to seeing you again soon.

With highest respect,
Kentaro Azumi
(1996.10)

Indian Letter Example

Vikram Singh
(address)

5 December 1996

Prof. K. Salazar
(address)

Respected Professor,

Salutations !

Please accept my humble apologies for not submitting the completed
course write-ups at the designated time. I am sure it has caused you
considerable inconvenience. Please find enclosed with this letter the
completed documents.

On the occasion of the impending festivities, I wish you all happiness.

Your servant,

Vikram Singh

Vikram Singh

Example I2   Writing Samples of the European Audience

French Style

Unlike businesses in most cultures, French human resource personnel may prefer a handwritten cover letter in the job search. Some businesses perform grapho-analysis on the handwriting sample as part of the screening process. When in doubt, call and ask.

French business letters show more formality than the U.S. style and less than the Asian style. For example, a French letter might begin, "I permit myself to introduce myself to you on behalf of Mr. Lefarge." At the end of a letter, you may see, "I ask of you to accept the expression of my distinguished consideration." In many French letters, you will notice the "we" orientation.

French Letter Example

BANQUE DU NORD

Viluniu Branch, Vytauto prospektas 17, Lithuania

Kazimiera Egliene
President
LitPex Bank
Paris

December 5, 1996

Re: Line of Credit

Dear Madam,

We are glad to inform you that Banque du Nord is opening a new branch in Vilnius. We look forward to cooperation with your respected bank as we start our operations.

Banque du Nord plans to be involved in money market transactions in domestic currency. With respect to this, we would like to ask your good bank to open a line of credit for us in the amount of LTL 10 million.

We would prefer to learn of your decision as soon as possible.

We remain yours faithfully,

J.P. Le Lapin
Financial Manager

British Style

The British may use humor or sarcasm in their everyday communication. In addition, they typically state facts in a roundabout way. For example, on her birthday celebration, which followed a year of family troubles chronicled in lurid detail by the nation's tabloid press, the Queen wrote these words: "1992 will not be a year on which I shall look with undiluted pleasure." Indeed.

Sir Winston Churchill loved to poke fun at language rules. In an oft-quoted excerpt from one of his letters, Churchill commented on "silly" strictures that govern English usage, specifically the rule that states, "Do not end a sentence with a preposition." Churchill's reply: "That is a rule up with which we shall not put!"

British Memorandum Example

Date: April 4, 1996
From: Timothy Peacocke
Subject: COMPANY PICNIC
To: Finance Group

Please be advised that this message was composed after a hideous financial audit. Please inject the following with your own bits of warm and fuzzy enthusiasm!

This is your last chance to get a ticket to the picnic. It's only $5.00. I know you have a lot of work to do, but it promises to be a good time. Drop your check into Anthony Mook's (pronounced like "book") mailbox. Come on out and enjoy the sun, friends, and good food!

Example I3   Writing Sample of the Latino Audience

Latino Style

Somewhat formal, the Latino style of writing is usually quite detailed. The following example thanks a business patron for sponsoring an indigent child in Santo Domingo.

Latino Letter Sample

ASOCIACION SANTO DOMINGO SAVIO

Project #0222

Dear Honored Sponsor, Mr. Nelson Alvarez,

We want to manifest our feelings of thankfulness for the great support you have given to Fabio Nelson Alvarez Alvarez.

The "Asociacion Santo Domingo Savio" is carrying out programs on Recreation, Personal Growth, Recycling, Psychology, and Dental Health aiming to meet the objectives which in one or another way will benefit the enrolled children, their families and the whole community.

[The middle section of the letter details each program.]

We hope to continue with these programs and services and, even more, improve them in order to meet the real needs of the community.

With the assurance that your support has really made it possible to improve the living conditions in our community, we remain gratefully yours.

Attentively,

Maria Santiago

Asociacion Santo Domingo Savio
Directive Board

Example I4   Writing Sample of the African Audience

African Style

In Africa, business writing will emphasize the relationship between two individuals. Greetings tend to be somewhat stylized and vary from country to country.

African FAX Example

To: Ms. Chelle Izzy, Director, African Trade Center, Washington D.C.
FAX # XX XXX XXX XXXX
From: Dr. Noboro Mufasa, Director, Department of Trade and
      Industry, Pretoria
Subject: S.A. Investment Conference
Date: January 12, 1996

Greetings,

How did you wake? Well, I hope. My wife sends her greetings to your family.

I need to discuss a matter of great importance. As you know, we are sponsoring the 18th Annual South African Investment Conference in Johannesburg in February. Will you or your representative be attending? We want to make the necessary arrangements for your safe transport and comfortable lodging.

The Conference on Africa's Development Challenges there in Washington was a most helpful meeting. Mr. Molefi Asante from our offices attended and has thoroughly briefed us on the various discussions. I believe the sponsorship of the World Bank brought a greater participation than we might have expected otherwise, and we hope for great things at our own conference here in Johannesburg.

We look forward to your response, as we continue to make our plans. Until we meet again, go well.

WRITING EVALUATION FORM

WRITER:

SUBJECT:

WRITER'S TARGET AUDIENCE: EVALUATOR:

CONTENT:
* Uses appropriate content for language comprehension of reader
* Seeks to establish relationship for high-context culture
* Shows evidence of research/understanding of subject
* Employs direct/indirect style as appropriate for reader

Strengths: **Needs Work:**

ORGANIZATION:
* Employs effective opening/closing
* Shows clear purpose in writing
* Expresses thoughts fluently using effective transitions
* Limits number of key points

Strengths: **Needs Work:**

PRESENTATION:
* Uses language correctly (grammar, usage, spelling)
* Employs effective spacing
* Explains statistics or lists with graphs, charts, or bullets
* Avoids two-word verbs and idioms

Strengths: **Needs Work:**

Overall Comments:

APPENDIX K

GUIDELINES FOR INCLUSIVE LANGUAGE

Inclusive language is language that does not *exclude* a reader or listener in any way.

The most common business mistakes regarding inclusive language are the use of the word *he* as a generic pronoun and the word *man* as a generic term for human being. These guidelines will help you avoid exclusive and inappropriate word choices.

"HE" AS A GENERIC PRONOUN

In general, avoid *he/she* and *s/he* entirely. Use *he or she* and *her or him* only when absolutely necessary.

Try one of these replacements in a sentence such as *Every worker must wear his or her hard-hat:*

- Convert to plural. *All workers must wear their hard-hats.*
- Use second person. *Wear your hard-hat.*
- Replace the pronoun (he) with an article (a, an, or the). *Each worker must wear a hard-hat.*

"MAN" AS A GENERIC TERM FOR HUMAN BEING

Replacing the generic *man* is not always as easy. For example, referring to a *manhole cover* to *personhole cover* is ridiculous, and *sewer-hole cover* is not much better.

Consider these four categories of language:

- Words that exclude women, such as *chairman* and *policeman*. Use words such as leader and police officer.
- Words that exclude men, such as *stewardess* and *actress*. Use words such as flight attendant and actor.
- Words that collectively include men and women but imply only men, such as *manpower* and *forefathers*. Use words such as *human resources* and *ancestors*.
- Words that call inappropriate attention to the person, such as *lady lawyer, female construction supervisor,* or *male nurse.*

Make titles, names of positions or occupations, and common references gender inclusive. Here are some examples, many of which are actually more specific than the inappropriate version:

Avoid	Revised
businessman	worker, manager, executive
coed	student
congressman	congressional representative
delivery man	delivery driver
draftsman	drafter
firemen	firefighter
foreman	supervisor
housewife	homemaker
husband, wife	spouse
mailman	mail carrier, letter carrier
man-hours	staff-hours
mankind	human beings, humanity, people
man-made	manufactured, artificial, synthetic
manpower	staff, human resources
newsman	reporter
repairman	service technician
saleslady, salesman	sales associate, clerk, salesperson, sales representative
spokesman	representative, advocate, spokesperson
waiter, waitress	server
watchman	guard, security officer
workman	laborer, worker

APPENDIX
L

NATIONAL HOLIDAYS
FOR SELECTED COUNTRIES

Holidays will affect the timing of your communication. In most cultures, expect to delay the delivery of your message for the time before and after important holidays.

AFRICAN HOLIDAYS

ALGERIA

January 1—New Year's Day
May 1—Labor Day
June 19—Ben Bella's Overthrow
July 5—Independence Day
November 1—Anniversary of the Revolution
   Variable: Muslim religious holidays

ANGOLA

January 1—New Year's Day
May 1—Labor Day
November 11—National Day
December 25—Christmas

EGYPT

January 1—New Year's Day
May 1—Labor Day
June 18—Evacuation Day
July 23—Revolution Day
October 6—Armed Forces Day
October 24—Popular Resistance Day
December 23—Victory Day
   Variable: Muslim religious holidays; Coptic Christian holidays; Mouloud, Birth of Muhammad (August)
   Optional: January 7 Coptic Christmas

NIGERIA

January 1—New Year's Day
October 1—National Day
December 25—Christmas

> Variable: Muslim religious holidays, Second Monday in March, Good Friday, Easter Monday

SOUTH AFRICA

January 1—New Year's Day
April 6—Founder's Day
May 1—Worker's Day
May 31—Republic Day
October 10—Kruger Day
December 16—Day of the Vow
December 25—Christmas
December 26—Day of Goodwill

> Variable: Good Friday, Family Day, Ascension Day
>
> Regional: January 2 (in the Western Cape)

ASIAN HOLIDAYS

CHINA

Chinese New Year—Celebrated for three days based on the lunar calendar
March 8—International Women's Day
May 1—Labor Day
August 1—Army Day
September 9—Teacher's Day
October 1,2—China's National Days

HONG KONG

December 25—Christmas

> Variable: Lunar New Year's Day, Ching Ming Festival, Easter, Dragon Boat Festival, Liberation Day, Chung Yeung Festival

INDIA

January 1—New Year's Day
March 17—St. Patrick's Day
December 25—Christmas

JAPAN

January 1—New Year's Day
January 15—Coming of Age Day
February 11—National Foundation Day
March 21—Vernal Equinox
April 29—Greenery Day
May 3—Constitution Memorial Day
May 4—People's Holiday
May 5—Children's Day
September 15—Respect for the Aged Day
September 23—Autumnal Equinox
October 10—Health Sports Day
November 3—Cultural Day
November 23—Labor Thanksgiving Day
December 23—Emperor's Birthday

KOREA, REPUBLIC OF

January 1,2—New Year's Day
March 1—Independence Movement Day
April 5—Arbor Day
May 5—Children's Day
June 6—Memorial Day
July 17—Constitution Day
August 15—Liberation Day
October 1—Armed Forces Day
October 3—National Foundation Day
October 9—Hangul, or Korean Alphabet Day
December 25—Christmas

> Variable: Lunar New Year's Day (Solnal), Buddha's Birthday (April, May), Choo Suk, Korean Thanksgiving Day (September)

SINGAPORE

January 1—New Year's Day
May 1—Labor Day
August 9—National Day
December 25—Christmas

> Variable: Chinese New Year, Good Friday, Vesak Day, Hari Raya, Puasa, Hari Raya Haji, Deepavali

TAIWAN

January 1,2—Founding Day of the Republic of China
March 29—Youth Day
April 5—Anniversary of President Chiang Kai-shek's Passing
September 28—Teacher's Day, Confucius' Birthday
October 10—National Day
October 25—Taiwan Retrocession Day
October 31—President Chiang Kai-shek's Birthday
November 12—Dr. Sun Yat-sen's Birthday
December 25—Constitution Day

> Variable: Lunar New Year, Lantern Festival, Dragon Boat Festival, Mid-Autumn Moon Festival

THAILAND

January 1—New Year's Day
April 6—Memorial Day, Chakri Day
April 13—Songkran Day
August 12—Queen's Birthday
October 23—Chulalongkorn Day
December 5—King's Birthday
December 10—Constitution Day
December 31—New Year's Eve

> Variable: Chinese New Year, Makhabuja (February), Coronation Day (May), Ploughing Ceremony (May), Visakhabuja (May, June), Asalhabuja (July), Beginning of Buddhist Lent (July)

EUROPEAN HOLIDAYS

AUSTRIA

January 1—New Year's Day
January 6—Epiphany
May 1—Labor Day
August 15—Assumption
October 26—National Holiday
November 1—All Saint's Day
December 8—Immaculate Conception
December 25—Christmas
December 26—St. Stephen's Day

  Variable: Easter Monday, Whit Monday, Corpus Christi

CANADA

January 1—New Year's Day
July 1—Canada Day
November 11—Remembrance Day
December 25—Christmas
December 26—Boxing Day

  Variable: Good Friday, Easter Monday, Victoria Day (May), Labor Day (September), Thanksgiving (October)

  Regional: First Monday in August, Heritage Day (in Alberta); first Monday in August, British Columbia Day (in British Columbia); first Monday in August, Civic Holiday (in Manitoba); second Monday in March, Commonwealth Day; March 17, St. Patrick's Day; April 24, St. George's Day; June 24, Discovery Day; July 1, Memorial Day; July 12, Orangemen's Day (in Newfoundland); first Monday in August, Civic Holiday (in Ontario); June 24, Fete National (in Quebec); first Monday in August, Civic Holiday (in Saskatchewan); third Monday in August, Discovery Day (in Yukon Territory); first Monday in August, Civic Holiday (in Northwest Territory)

FRANCE

Many people are on vacation between mid-July and mid-September.

January 1—New Year's Day
May 1—Labor Day
May 8—Armistice 1945
July 14—Bastille Day
August 15—Assumption
November 1—All Saint's Day
November 11—Memorial Day
December 25—Christmas

    Variable: Easter Monday, Ascension Day, Whitmonday

GERMANY

January 1—New Year's Day
May 1—Labor Day
October 3—German Unity Day
November 18—Day of Repentance and Prayer
December 25—Christmas
December 26—Boxing Day

    Variable: Good Friday, Easter Monday, Ascension Thursday, Whit Monday

    Regional: Epiphany (in Baden-Wurttemberg and Bayern); Corpus Christi (in Baden-Wurttemberg, Bayern, Hessen, Nordrhein-Westfalen, Rheinland-Pfalz, Saarland); Assumption of the Blessed Virgin (in parts of Bayern, Saarland); October 31, Reformation Day (in Brandenburg, Mecklenburg-Vorpommern, Sachsen, Sachsen-Ahnalt, Thuringen); All Saint's Day (in Baden-Wurttemberg, Bayern, Nordrhein-Westfalen, Rheinland-Pfalz, Saarland, parts of Thuringen)

IRELAND

January 1—New Year's Day
March 17—St. Patrick's Day
December 25—Christmas
December 26—St. Stephen's Day

    Variable: Good Friday; Easter Monday; the First Monday in June, bank holiday; the First Monday in August, bank holiday; the Last Monday in October, bank holiday

ITALY

Many people are on vacation between mid-July and mid-September.

January 1—New Year's Day
January 6—Epiphany
April 25—Liberation Day
May 1—Labor Day
August 15—Assumption of the Virgin
November 1—All Saint's Day
December 8—Immaculate Conception
December 25—Christmas
December 26—Santo Stefano

    Variable: Good Friday, Easter Monday

UNITED KINGDOM

Queen's Birthday observed on a Saturday in June. Businesses not affected. The spring and summer holidays, often called bank holidays, are observed by all businesses.

ENGLAND, WALES, SCOTLAND

January 1—New Year's Day
December 25—Christmas

    Variable: Good Friday; Easter Monday; May Day (May), Spring Holiday or bank holiday (May), Summer holiday or bank holiday (August), Boxing Day (December), the day after Boxing Day (December)

NORTHERN IRELAND

January 1—New Year's Day
March 17—St. Patrick's Day
July 22—Orangemen's Day
December 25—Christmas

LATINO HOLIDAYS

ARGENTINA

January 1—New Year's Day
May 1—Labor Day
May 25—Revolution Day
June 10—Sovereignty Day
June 20—Flag Day
July 9—Independence Day
August 17—Death of San Martin
October 12—Columbus Day
December 8—Virgin's Day
December 25—Christmas
December 31—New Year's Eve

> Variable: Holy Thursday, Good Friday

BRAZIL

Businesspeople in Brazil are most likely to be on vacation in February, the first two weeks in March, July, and the end of December.

January 1—New Year's Day
April 21—Tiradentes Day
May 1—Labor Day
September 7—Independence Day
November 2—All Soul's Day
November 15—Proclamation of the Republic
December 8—Immaculate Conception
December 25—Christmas
December 26—Day after Christmas

> Variable: Carnival (two weeks in February or March), Ash Wednesday (half day), Good Friday, Easter Saturday, Easter Monday, Corpus Christi, Our Lady Appeared (October)

> Regional: January 20, Founding of Rio de Janeiro (in Rio de Janeiro); January 25, Founding of São Paulo (in São Paulo)

> Optional: Holy Thursday; November 1, All Saint's Day

CHILE

January 1—New Year's Day
May 1—Labor Day
May 21—Commemoration of the Battle of Iquique
August 15—Assumption Day
September 11—National Day
September 18—Independence Day
September 19—Armed Force's Day
October 12—Columbus Day
November 1—All Saint's Day
December 8—Immaculate Conception
December 25—Christmas

Variable: Good Friday, Easter Saturday, Corpus Christi

COLOMBIA

Vacations are taken in December, January, June, and July.

January 1—New Year's Day
January 6—Epiphany
May 1—Labor Day
June 9—Thanksgiving
June 29—SS. Peter and Paul
July 20—Colombia Independence Day
August 7—Battle of Boyaca
August 15—Assumption Day
October 12—Columbus Day
November 1—All Saint's Day
November 11—Independence of Cartagena
December 8—Immaculate Conception
December 25—Christmas

Variable: St. Joseph's Day (March), Holy Thursday, Good Friday, Ascension Thursday, Corpus Christi

Optional: Feast of Sacred Heart and SS. Peter and Paul

COSTA RICA

January 1—New Year's Day
March 19—Saint Joseph's Day
April 11—Battle of Rivas
May 1—Labor Day
June 29—SS. Peter and Paul
July 25—Annexation of the Province of Guanacaste
August 2—Festivity of Our Lady of the Angels
August 15—Mother's Day
September 15—Independence Day
October 12—Columbus Day
December 8—Festivity of the Immaculate Conception
December 25—Christmas

Variable: Holy Thursday, Good Friday, Corpus Christi

ECUADOR

January 1—New Year's Day
May 1—Labor Day
May 24—Battle of Pichincha
July 24—Bolivar's Birthday
August 10—Independence Day
October 9—Independence of Guayaquil
October 12—Columbus Day
November 1—All Saint's Day
November 2—All Soul's Day
November 3—Independence of Cuenca
December 6—Founding of Quito
December 25—Christmas

Variable: Carnival Day, Holy Thursday, Good Friday

Regional: Founding of Guayaquil (in Guayaquil only)

GUATEMALA

January 1—New Year's Day
January 6—Epiphany
May 1—Labor Day
June 30—Anniversary of the Revolution

September 15—Independence Day
October 12—Columbus Day
October 20—Revolution Day
November 1—All Saint's Day
December 25—Christmas
December 26—Day after Christmas
December 31—New Year's Eve

    Variable: Good Friday, Easter

    Regional: August 15, Assumption of the Virgin (in Guatemala City only)

MEXICO

Mexico does not move holidays to the beginning or end of the week.

January 1—New Year's Day
February 5—Anniversary of Mexican Constitution
March 21—Juarez's Birthday
May 5—Anniversary of the Battle of Puebla
September 1—President's State of the Union Address
September 16—Independence Day
October 12—Dia de la Raza (Columbus Day)
November 2—Day of the Dead
November 20—Mexican Revolution
December 25—Christmas

    Variable: Holy Thursday, Good Friday

    Optional: December 12, Our Lady of Guadalupe

PERU

January 1—New Year's Day
May 1—Labor Day
June 29—SS. Peter and Paul
July 28—Independence Day
August 30—St. Rosa of Lima
October 8—Battle of Angamos
November 1—All Saint's Day
December 8—Immaculate Conception
December 25—Christmas

    Variable: Maundy Thursday, Good Friday

PORTUGAL

January 1—New Year's Day
April 25—Liberty Day
May 1—Labor Day
June 10—Portugal Day
August 15—Assumption of the Virgin
October 5—Proclamation of the Republic
November 1—All Saint's Day
December 1—Restoration of Independence
December 8—Immaculate Conception
December 25—Christmas

> Variable: Carnival Day, Shrove Tuesday, Good Friday, Corpus Christi

> Regional: June 13, St. Anthony (in Lisbon only); June 24, St. John the Baptist (in Porto only)

SPAIN

January 1—New Year's Day
January 6—Epiphany
May 1—St. Joseph the Workman
July 25—St. James of Campostela
August 15—Assumption
October 12—Day of Spain
November 1—All Saint's Day
December 6—Constitution Day
December 8—Immaculate Conception
December 25—Christmas

> Variable: Maundy Thursday, Good Friday, Easter Monday, Corpus Christi

> Regional: May 15, St. Isidro (in Madrid)

VENEZUELA

January 1—New Year's Day
April 19—Declaration of Independence
May 1—Labor Day
June 24—Battle of Carabobo
July 5—Independence Day
July 24—Simon Bolivar's Birthday, Battle of Logo de Maracaibo

September 4—Civil Servants' Day

October 12—Columbus Day

December 24—Christmas

Variable: Carnival, Holy Thursday, Good Friday

Regional: March 10 (in La Guiara only), October 24 (in Maracaibo only)

Optional: January 6, Epiphany; March 19, St. Joseph; June 29, SS. Peter and Paul; August 15, Assumption Day; November 1, All Saint's Day; December 8, Immaculate Conception

BIBLIOGRAPHY

Aburdene, Patricia and Naisbitt, John. *MegaTrends for Women: From Liberation to Leadership*. New York: Fawcett Columbine, 1992.

Ailes, R., with Kraushar, J. *You Are the Message*. Homewood, IL: Dow Jones-Irwin, 1988.

Aries, E. "Gender and Communication." P. Shaver and C. Hendrick (eds.). *Sex and Gender*. Newbury Park, CA: Sage Publications, 1987, pp. 149–176.

Austin, Nancy K. "Managing by Parable," *Working Woman*, September 1995, pp. 14–16.

Axtell, Roger E. *The Do's and Taboos Around the World*, 3rd ed. New York: John Wiley & Sons, 1993.

Axtell, Roger E. *The Do's and Taboos of International Trade*, rev. ed. New York: John Wiley & Sons, 1994.

Baird, J. E. and Bradley, P. H. "Styles of Management and Communication: A Comparative Study of Men and Women." *Communication Monographs*. Vol 46, 1979, pp. 101–111.

Ball, Donald A., and McCullough, Wendell, H. Jr. *International Business: Introduction and Essentials*. 5th ed. Homewood, IL: Irwin, 1993.

Barton, Laurence. *Crisis in Organizations: Managing and Communicating in the Heat of Chaos*. Cincinnati, OH: SouthWestern, 1993.

Beamer, Linda, and Varner, Iris. *Intercultural Communication in the Global Workplace*. Homewood, IL: Irwin, 1995.

Beamer, Linda. "Learning Intercultural Communication Competence." *The Journal of Business Communication*. Vol. 29, No. 3, 1992, p. 285.

Begley, Sharon. "Gray Matters: New Technologies That Catch the Mind in the Very Act of Thinking Show How Men and Women Use Their Brains Differently." *Newsweek*. March 20, 1995.

Bell, Ella L. "The Bicultural Life Experience of Career-Oriented Black Women." *Journal of Organizational Behavior*. Vol. 11, 1990, pp. 459–477.

Bell, Ella L., and Nkomo, S. M. "Revisioning Women Managers' Lives." *Gendering Organizational Analysis*. Newbury Park, CA: Sage, 1992, pp. 235–247.

Beyer, Lisa, "Life Behind the Veil." *Time: Special Edition*. Vol. 136, No. 19, Fall 1990, p. 37.

Boone, Louis E., and Kurtz, David L. *Contemporary Business Communication*. Englewood Cliffs, NJ: Prentice Hall, 1994.

Buffett, Warren. Address to the Kenan-Flagler Business School, The University of North Carolina at Chapel Hill, PBS broadcast, August 15, 1995.

Calas, Marta B. and Smircich, Linda. "Dangerous Liaisons: The 'Feminine-in-Management' Meets 'Globalization'." *Business Horizons*. Vol. 36, No. 2, March 1993, p. 71.

Carr-Ruffino, Norma. *Managing Cultural Differences*. Cincinnati, OH: Thomson Executive Press, 1996.

Carr-Ruffino, Norma. *The Promotable Woman*. Belmont, CA: Wadsworth, 1993.

Carson, Kerry D., Carson, Paula Phillips, and Irwin, Charles. "Enhancing Communication and Interactional Effectiveness with Mexican-American Trainees." *Business Communication Quarterly*. Vol. 58, No. 3, September 1995, p. 19.

Catlin, Linda, and White, Thomas. *International Business: Cultural Sourcebook and Case Studies*. Cincinnati, OH: SouthWestern, 1994.

Chaney, Lillian H., and Martin, Jeanette S. *Intercultural Business Communication*. Englewood Cliffs, NJ: Prentice Hall, 1995.

Copeland, Lennie, and Griggs, Lewis. *Going International: How to Make Friends and Deal Effectively in the Global Marketplace*. New York: Random House, 1985.

Copeland, Lennie. "Learning to Manage a Multicultural Workplace." *The Magazine of Human Resource Development*. May 1988, pp. 48–56.

Copeland, Lennie. "Savoir Faire Over There." *Nation's Business*. September 1986, p. 48.

Copeland, Lennie, and Griggs, Lewis, *Going International: How to Make Friends and Deal Effectively in the Global Marketplace*. New York: Random House, 1992.

Deaux, K., "Sex and Gender," *Annual Review of Psychology*. Vol. 36, 1985, pp. 49–81.

DeVilliers, Les, Marais, Jan, and Wiehahn, Nic (eds). *Doing Business with South Africa*. New Canaan, CT: Business Books International, 1986.

Dodd, Carley H. *Dynamics of Intercultural Communication*, 3rd ed. New York: William C. Brown, 1991.

DuBrin, A. J., "Sex and Gender Differences in Tactics of Influence." *Psychological Reports*. Vol. 68, 1991, pp. 635–646.

Duffy, Margaret, "Do You Hear What I Hear?" *Entrepreneurial Woman*. Jan/Feb 1991, pp. 54–57.

Dyson, Michael Eric. *Between God and Gangsta Rap: Bearing Witness to Black Culture*. Chapel Hill, NC: Oxford Press, 1995.

Eagly, A. H., and Johnson, V. J. "Gender and Leadership Style: A Meta-Analysis," *Psychology Bulletin*. Vol. 108, 1990, pp. 233–256.

Eiben, Therese. "If You Can't Join 'Em, Beat 'Em." *Fortune*. September 21, 1992, p. 50.

Ekman, Paul, and Friesen, Wallace V. "The International Language of Gestures." *Psychology Today*, May 1984, pp. 64–69.

Ellyson, Steve L., Dovidio, John F., and Brown, Clifford E. "The Look of Power: Gender Differences and Similarities in Visual Behavior." *Gender, Interaction, and Inequality*. C. Ridgeway (ed.). New York: Springer-Verlag, 1992, pp. 50–80.

Engholm, Christopher. *Doing Business in Asia's Booming China Triangle*. Englewood Cliffs, NJ: Prentice Hall, 1994.

Fagenson, E. A. (ed.). *Women in Management: Trends, Issues, and Challenges in Managerial Diversity*. Newbury Park, CA: Sage, 1993.

Fortner, Robert S. *International Communication: History, Conflict, and Control of the Global Metropolis*. Belmont, CA: Wadsworth, 1993.

Gardner III, William L., Peluchette, Joy Van Eck, and Clinebell, Sharon K. "Valuing Women in Management: An Impression Management Perspective of Gender Diversity" *Management Communication Quarterly*. Vol. 8, No. 2, November 1994, pp.115–164.

Gilligan, C. *In a Different Voice: Psychological Theory and Women's Development*. Cambridge, MA: Harvard University Press, 1982.

Goldman, Alan. *Doing Business With the Japanese: A Guide to Successful Communication, Management, and Diplomacy*. Albany, NY: State University of New York Press, 1994.

Gorman, Christine. "Sizing Up the Sexes: Scientists Are Discovering that Gender Differences Have as Much to Do with the Biology of the Brain as with the Way We Are Raised." *Time*. Vol. 139, No. 3, January 20, 1982, p. 42.

Grauer, Robert T., and Barber, Maryann. *Exploring Microsoft PowerPoint*. Englewood Cliffs, NJ: Prentice Hall, 1994.

Guffy, Mary Ellen. *Business Communication: Process and Product*. Belmont, CA: Wadsworth, 1994.

Hamlin, Sonya. *How To Talk So People Listen*. New York: Harper & Row, 1988.

Harcourt, J., Krizan, A. C., Merrier, P. *Business Communication*, 3rd ed. Cincinnati, OH: International Thomson Publishing, 1996.

Harris, Collingwood. "Women as Managers." *Working Woman*. November 1995, p. 14.

Haywood, Richette L., "Can Myrlie Evers-Williams save the NAACP?" *Ebony*, October 1995, pp. 38–42, 142.

Hect, Michael L., and others. *African American Communication*. Newbury Park, CA: Sage Publications, 1995.

Herbert, R. K. "Sex-Based Differences in Compliment Behavior." *Language in Society*. Vol.19, 1990, pp. 201–224.

Hill, Charles W. L. *International Business*. Boston: Irwin, 1994.

Holtgraves, T. "Interpreting Questions and Replies: Effects of Face-Threat, Question Form, and Gender" *Social Psychology Quarterly*. Vol. 54, 1991, pp. 15–24.

Hynson, Larry M. *Doing Business with South Korea*. New York: Quorum Books, 1990.

Jacobs, J. A. "Women's Entry into Management: Trends in Earnings, Authority, and Values Among Salaried Managers." *Administrative Science Quarterly*. June 1992, pp. 282–301.

Jessup, Jay M., and Maggie, L. *Doing Business in Mexico*. Rocklin, CA: Prima Publishing, 1993.

Kenton, Sherron B. "Speaker Credibility in Persuasive Business Communication: A Model Which Explains Gender Differences." *The Journal of Business Communication*. Vol. 26, No. 2, Spring 1989, p. 143.

Kenton, Sherron B. "The Gender Gap in Business." *Georgia Trend*. Vol. 4, No. 3, November 1988, p. 65.

Kenton, Sherron B. "Gender Credibility Issue Affects All." *The Daily News*. March 24, 1991.

Klopf, Donald. *Intercultural Encounter*. 2nd ed. Colorado: Morton Publishing, 1991.

Kurtzig, Sandra L. "In Man's World." *ComputerWorld*. March 21, 1994.

Lakoff, Robin. *Language and Woman's Place*. New York: Harper & Row, 1975.

Lakoff, Robin. "What You Can Do with Words: Politeness, Pragmatics, and Performatives." *Berkeley Studies in Syntax and Semantics*. Vol. 16, 1974, pp. 1–55.

Lowe, Doug. *PowerPoint 4 for Windows for Dummies*. San Mateo, CA: IDG Books, 1994.

Lusardi, Lee A. "When A Woman Speaks, Does Anybody Listen?" *Working Woman*. July 1990, pp. 92–95.

Lustig, Myron, and Koester, Jolene. *Intercultural Competence: Interpersonal Communication Across Cultures*. New York: Harper Collins College Publishers, 1993.

Maddox, Robert C. *Cross-Cultural Problems in International Business: The Role of the Cultural Integration Function*. Westport, CT: Quorum Books, 1993.

McGeary, Johanna. "Challenge in the East: The Emerging Democracies Offer a Chance for Women to Share Real, Rather than Cosmetic, Power" *Time Special Edition*. Vol. 136, No. 19, Fall 1990, p. 30.

Mead, Richard. *Cross-Cultural Management Communication*. Chichester, England: John Wiley & Sons, 1990.

Mead, Richard. *International Management Cross-Cultural Dimensions*. Cambridge, MA: Blackwell, 1994.

Morrison, Terri, and others. *Kiss, Bow or Shake Hands*. Holbrook, MA: Bob Adams, 1994.

Munger, Susan H. *The International Business Communications Desk Reference*. New York: Amacom, 1993.

Munter, Mary. *Business Communication: Strategy and Skill*. Englewood Cliffs, NJ: Prentice-Hall, 1987.

Munter, Mary. *Guide to Managerial Communication*, 3rd ed. Englewood Cliffs, NJ: Prentice Hall, 1992.

Noble, Barbara Presley. "Do Men and Women Lead Differently?" *The New York Times*, August 15, 1993.

Ober, Scot. *Contemporary Business Communication*. Boston, MA: Houghton Mifflin, 1995.

Ochs, Elinor, "Indexing Gender." *Rethinking Context: Language as an Interactive Phenomenon*. A. Duranti and C. Goodwin (eds.). Cambridge, England: Cambridge University, 1992, pp. 335–358.

O'Hara-Devereaux, Mary, and Johansen, Robert. *Globalwork: Bridging Distance, Culture, and Time*. San Francisco: Jossey-Bass, 1994.

Phatak, Arvind V. *International Dimensions of Management*, 4th ed. Cincinnati, OH: SouthWestern, 1995.

Powell, G. N. *Women and Men in Management*. Newbury Park, CA: Sage,1993.

Powell, G.N., "One More Time: Do Female and Male Managers Differ?" *The Executive*. Vol. IV, No. 3, August 1990, p. 68.

"Precision Language: Saying What We Mean." *Advancing Philanthropy*, Summer 1995.

Reich, Robert B. *The Work of Nations*. New York: Vintage, 1992.

Rossman, Marlene L. *The International Businesswoman of the 1990s*. New York: Praeger Press, 1990.

Rudolph, Barbara, "Why Can't a Woman Manage More Like...A Woman?" *Time Special Edition*. Vol. 136, No. 19, Fall 1990, p. 53.

Samovar, Larry A., and Porter, Richard R. *Intercultural Communication: A Reader*. Cincinnati, OH: International Thomson Publishing, 1994.

Saravia-Shore, Marietta, and Arvizu, Steven F. *Cross-Cultural Literacy: Ethnographies of Communication in Multiethnic Classrooms*. New York: Garland Publishing, 1992.

Scheele, Adele. *Career Strategies for Women*. New York: Simon & Schuster, 1994.

Steele, Carolyn Odom. "African-American Women Network Their Way to the Top." *Executive Female*, May/June 1995, pp. 38–39, 75.

Stewart, Lea, Alan-Friedley, Sheryl, and Cooper, Pamela J. *Communication Between the Sexes*. Scottsdale, AZ: Gorsuch Scarisbrick, 1990.

Tannen, Deborah. *Talking 9 to 5*. New York: William Morrow, 1994.

Tannen, Deborah. *You Just Don't Understand*. New York: William Morrow, 1990.

Terpstra, Vern, and David, Kenneth. *The Cultural Environment of International Business*. Cincinnati, OH: SouthWestern Publishing, 1991.

Thiederman, Sondra B. *Bridging Cultural Barriers for Corporate Success: How to Manage the Multicultural Work Force*. Lexington, MA: Lexington Books, 1991.

Thiederman, Sondra. *Profiting in America's Multicultural Workplace*. New York: Lexington Books, 1991.

Thorne, B., Kramara, C., and Henley, N. *Language, Gender and Society*. Rowley, MA: Newbury House,1983.

Timm, Paul, and Stead, James. *Communication for Business and Professions*. Englewood Cliffs, NJ: Prentice Hall, 1996.

Ting-Toomey, Stella, and Korzenny, Felipe. "Cross-Cultural Interpersonal Communication." *International and Intercultural Communication Annual*, Vol. XV, Newbury Park, CA: Sage, 1991.

Ting-Toomey, Stella. *The Challenge of Facework: Cross-Cultural and Interpersonal Issues*. Albany, NY: State University of New York Press, 1994.

Trompenaars, Fons. *Riding The Waves of Culture: Understanding Diversity in Global Business*. BurrRidge, IL: Irwin, 1994.

Tuller, Lawrence W. *Doing Business in Latin America and the Caribbean*. New York: American Management Association, 1993.

Turner, Patricia A. *I Heard it Through the Grapevine*. Los Angeles: University of California Press, 1995.

Varner, Iris, and Beamer, Linda. *Intercultural Communication in the Global Workplace*. Chicago: Irwin, 1995.

Victor, David. *International Business Communication*. New York: Harper Collins, 1992.

Yamada, Haru. *American and Japanese Business Discourse*. Vol. XLV. Norwood, NJ: Ablex Publishing, 1992.

INDEX